YOU, ME & ADHD

SAM THOMPSON

PUFFIN

PUFFIN BOOKS

UK | USA | Canada | Ireland | Australia
India | New Zealand | South Africa

Puffin Books is part of the Penguin Random House group of companies
whose addresses can be found at global.penguinrandomhouse.com.
www.penguin.co.uk   www.puffin.co.uk   www.ladybird.co.uk

Penguin
Random House
UK

First published 2026
002

Text copyright © Sam Thompson, 2026
Illustrations copyright © Helen Green, 2026

The moral right of the author and illustrator has been asserted

This book shares the author's personal experiences of living with ADHD, along with
ideas and strategies that have worked for him. The information in this book is for
general purposes and should not be relied on for medical advice. If you have any
questions or concerns about ADHD, or about your own or your child's health, you
should seek advice from a qualified healthcare professional.

Design & layout by Dynamo Limited
Decorative artwork © Adobe Stock

Printed in Great Britain by Clays Ltd, Elcograf S.p.A

The authorized representative in the EEA is Penguin Random House Ireland,
Morrison Chambers, 32 Nassau Street, Dublin D02 YH68

A CIP catalogue record for this book is available from the British Library

ISBN: 978–0–241–82487–0

All correspondence to:
Puffin Books
Penguin Random House Children's
One Embassy Gardens,
8 Viaduct Gardens, London SW11 7BW

Penguin Random House is committed to a
sustainable future for our business, our readers
and our planet. This book is made from Forest
Stewardship Council® certified paper.

CONTENTS

INTRODUCTION

THE THING THAT MAKES YOU, YOU!

Hi. I'm Sam, nice to meet you!

Thank you so much for picking up my book. I'm really excited you're here, and I hope together we can go on a journey to discover more about what I like to call amazingly awesome ADHD.

Now, let's start at the very beginning, a very good place to start.

I was diagnosed with ADHD at the age of thirty – that's ancient! Discovering I had ADHD, or Attention Deficit Hyperactivity Disorder (although I'm not a fan of some of those words – more on this later . . .) was a huge turning point in my life. It also made a lot of sense. A lot of questions I've had my whole life about why I absolutely love doing some things and find other activities harder were suddenly answered. I've always felt different to other people but never knew exactly why. Since being a young kid, I've found some things hard – like studying some subjects at school, or how my bedroom can start to look like a rubbish bin if I don't stay on top of it and keep up my routine. But for other activities, like gaming on my PlayStation or hanging out with my cats, I feel like there just aren't enough hours in the day for me to devote to them . . .!

In fact, there are lots of things that come easily to me that others might struggle with. I am creative, and ideas come easily to me. I almost have too many ideas! I am resilient and bounce back from

disappointment, and I'm surprisingly good in a crisis. I also try to be kind every day. In some little way, I make an effort to help someone around me feel happy and better about themselves. Another strength is that I can talk at super-speed, and when I find something I am interested in (like Greek mythology!), I get sooo excited and pay attention to it for ages.

What about you? I am willing to bet millions of pounds on the fact that you have lots of things that are special about you, too.

But first, here comes the science bit, so we know we've got that covered. Because I have ADHD, my brain (and perhaps yours too, or someone you care about) works in a special way. Maybe you've heard this term before? It stands for 'Attention Deficit Hyperactivity Disorder'. That's quite the mouthful, isn't it! So for the rest of this book, let's just stick with ADHD *(ah-de-aich-dee)*. We'll zoom in and take a closer look at what this actually means very soon, but for now, I want to spend a bit more time thinking about our strengths.

Although I realize how difficult ADHD traits can be, I'm on a personal mission to highlight the positives and raise awareness about ADHD. And trust me, guys, there are so many positives! We all think and talk about our ADHD differently, and for me personally, I find that it helps me to explain it as my superpower. You might call it your superpower too, but other people and some grown-ups might prefer to think about their ADHD or difference in another way. I have always loved superheroes, though, especially Spider-Man, so it felt like an easy way for

me to understand and explain (if I wanted to) about my ADHD. I know I have challenges, but it has given me unique skills and talents that I'm so grateful for! How I see it, a superhero is someone a little bit different, with a few awesome skills that they try to use for good. So, if you see me talk about superheroes and superpowers a few times in this book, you now know why – it is how I choose to understand and talk about ADHD. I know that the superpower metaphor doesn't work for everyone, and I understand that, and would never want to downplay the challenges that can come with ADHD. But in my experience, my ADHD has given me a lot of strengths, and I like to focus on those positives. I hope this book will help you think about your special skills and talents, too!

In the book, I will sometimes talk about technology and some digital resources that have helped me. I understand not everyone will have things like laptops and tablets at home so please speak to a teacher or your local library about getting access to these.

There are two different brain types: neurotypical and neurodivergent. ADHD is a neurodivergent brain type that processes information in a specialised way. ADHD affects the functions of the brain that control concentration, emotion, organization, memory and more.

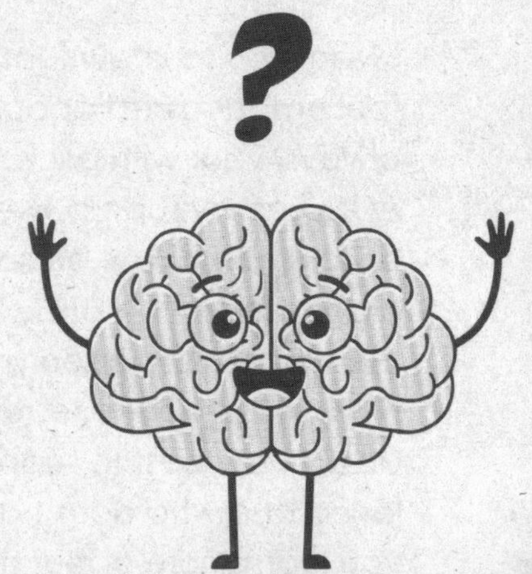

There are three different types of ADHD: inattentive, hyperactive/impulsive, and combined, which is the most common type of ADHD and the one I was diagnosed with. Someone with ADHD may struggle to sit still, stay organized, or accidentally forget things. But ADHD can come with some incredible strengths, as well as challenges. A person with ADHD will be AMAZINGLY AWESOME; it's just about making sure the differences in our brains are understood and celebrated. With different types of ADHD, they are on what is called a 'spectrum' of being neurodivergent. Because of this, it is possible that some symptoms of your ADHD may not be regulated by using tools found in this book. I would always recommend also talking to your parent/ caregiver, teacher and GP for additional support.

I want you to know that ADHD is nothing to hide or feel embarrassed about; it is something you should always wear with pride. That's why I talk about ADHD as my superpower, you see. You are an absolutely brilliant person, and if you have been diagnosed with ADHD, then your ADHD is a part of the wonderful person you are. And if you don't have it, but you're reading this book to learn more about how best to support and help a friend or loved one who does have it, then this book will help you learn more about how an ADHD brain works, and how you can understand and support this by being kind. Which you clearly are, since you picked up this book!

I was lucky enough to be diagnosed with my ADHD during a documentary and I was in a position to pay for private support to help me, afterwards. If you think you are neurodivergent, please talk to your teacher (or another trusted adult in school) and your caregiver to look into getting an assessment and diagnosis.

One thing I would love each person who reads this book to feel at the end is that you have had a bit of space and time to think about the things that you are really good at. I know from personal experience that being

diagnosed with ADHD can be a bit scary at first. It's natural to want to be the same as everyone else, but trust me, you are not alone. There are tons of us out there with different neurodivergent conditions, and the more we learn about how our amazingly awesome brains are wired, the more we know how to make sure we feel supported to shine.

It is a saying you may have heard before but everyone is different. There are also people who might not have ADHD but have a difference where they face different challenges to us.

I often feel different to other people, and sometimes I felt that way growing up too. I want you to know this difference came with unique skills and talents, and now I'm so grateful to be different. I honestly wouldn't have it any other way. My job in this book is to show you all the ways that you are awesome and amazing exactly as you are. Together, we'll look at the source of this awesomeness: your amazing brain. We all have a brain, and each one is totally unique, carrying our likes and dislikes, our memories, helping us decide what to do and what not to do. The differences in our brains should be recognized and appreciated. I want this book to be a safe space for you to discover all the things to celebrate about your unique brain, and the brains of your friends and loved ones. By the end of this book I hope you'll have learned some new strategies and techniques to help you feel as awesome as possible, and also some ideas for how to let other people know if you are ever finding things difficult, because sometimes all of us find things difficult, and that's OK, you just need to make sure you tell a trusted grown-up about it.

ADHD can mean more energy or increased creativity, and it can also mean that you sometimes need a toolbox of strategies to help you achieve your goals.

The first step is to work out what your goals are (no, not the goals you score on the football field or netball court!). I mean focusing in on what you really want, what you love and what you like. Otherwise, you might end up zimming-zooming all over the world without ever stopping to think whether this is the best use of your strengths. Or the opposite – you might keep really quiet and worry about revealing your skills at all. ADHD shows up in so many different ways in different people and can also change as you grow older.

Don't worry – I know it's a lot – but this is where I, and this book, come in. We're going to look at all of these things together and work it all out.

And it's important that we do. It is only by understanding ourselves that we can appreciate our strengths, rather than worrying about our differences and wasting time and energy wishing we could just be normal and not stand out.

But first, let's take a quick time-out to look at another big word you might have heard: **'neurodivergent'**.

NEURODIVERGENT

It is estimated that about twenty per cent of people around the world are **neurodivergent**. For example, in a class of twenty kids around four will may be neurodivergent. This means they have a brain that functions in a way that is considered 'non-typical'. Examples include autism, dyslexia, ADHD and many more conditions. I have so much respect for neurodivergents living with their diagnosed differences.

It's important to remember that all our brains are different and unique. One person's idea of 'normal' will be very different to someone else's, and each person experiences the world in their own way. The more scientists learn about our brains, the more it is being scientifically proven that there's no such thing as 'normal'. And thank goodness for that! Life would be very dull indeed if all our brains functioned in the same way.

Just like in the Marvel comics, where each superhero has a unique skill or talent they can use to make the world a better (or safer!) place, I firmly believe each person has their own special strengths. You might be amazing at drawing, for example, or a maths superstar, or a really great listener who always helps their friends. Just pause for a second now and have a little think about where your passions and your talents lie. Go on – write them down, perhaps under the heading 'Reasons why I am awesome!'.

But back to our Marvel superheroes. Our hero might know they have special skills that let them do things others can't, but they feel sad when they don't fit in. Having super-speed can be super-fun, but it can also feel super-chaotic. It can also feel lonely.

Luckily, there are lots of things you can do to help yourself feel less alone:

- See if you can find a **mentor** – a trusted adult with experience who can understand you and help others understand you, too. Ask your parents, carers or teacher for help finding the right person for you.

- Look to join a **club**. For me, this always meant sport, particularly my rugby and football teams at school. That feeling of belonging was a game-changer for me, and it can be for you, too. I've found that when a group of people with different skills fit together like puzzle pieces, they can achieve greater things and live a happier life filled with friendship and direction.

- Spend some time thinking about your **purpose** – the things you really love using your talents for. The aim is to direct your strengths towards things that make you feel good and proud.

For me, this is helping people like you! The purpose of this book – and for me, writing it – is to try to positively change people's view of ADHD and neurodiversity. I am also an ambassador for the charity ADHD UK, which means a lot to me.
I really want to encourage everyone, especially young people like you, to embrace all the ways your brilliant brain makes you different and unique, and to recognize that even though it might not feel like it at times, that difference can be powerful.

To do all of these things, the first thing you have to do is understand yourself.

TRY THIS

It's time for that pencil and piece of paper again. Don't worry, I'm not asking you to write an essay. What I do want you to do is try to answer a few questions:

What do **I love to do?**

I love to game with my mates . . .

What about me helps me to do that thing in a **special way**?

I have good hand-eye coordination and remember the shortcuts better than my mates!

How is my way **different** from other people's?

I sometimes get very focused on winning a game, and nothing can distract me. I keep going until I win!

And how can I **explain** that to people who sometimes take a bit longer to understand?

When I'm playing, I get really focused because my brain locks on to the goal. It helps me play well, but sometimes it means I need a moment before I can switch to something else.

You can come back to these questions and answer
them lots of times, to explore all the things you like
doing. When you see your answers written down,
hopefully they will help you spot what you're good
at, why, and how your way of doing things might
be different to other people's. All of this helps you
build up a picture of who you really are, and what
your strengths and challenges may be.

And this is important, because to me,
one of the things I've really struggled
with along the way – the same way
I think superheroes might feel
sometimes – is being *misunderstood*.

And in order to explain yourself to people
who don't understand you yet, you need to
be able to explain yourself to *you*.

I don't know if you have realized, but this whole
time I wasn't just talking about super-speed or
strength . . . I was also talking about ADHD.

You see, having ADHD is something that I feel proud
of. Or as I think of it, my superpower. It has let me
focus super-intensely on things I find interesting,
make some really awesome friends for life and think
in different, exciting and creative ways.

But sometimes it also made me feel different, and
occasionally, a bit lonely too.

What I've learned, though, is that it doesn't have to feel that way. I can make the good things about it better and the hard stuff easier if I take some time – and get a little bit of help – to understand how my brain works and explain it to the people around me. When I say the 'hard stuff', by the way, I mean things that frustrate me. How I sometimes struggle to concentrate on something important, or can get really upset with myself if someone is trying to be helpful and give me some feedback on something I may not have got right.

This book is that little bit of time and that little bit of help for you.

If you are anything like me, there will have been many times when you tried to do the right thing, but somehow the way you did it ended up making other people confused. Or cross.

Or . . .

Bright-red-in-the-face-WHY-CAN'T-YOU-JUST-DO-IT-LIKE-EVERYONE-ELSE?

. . . angry.

What I didn't have was a way to explain why
I didn't do things like everyone else.

Or a way to show people how I could do
something differently and well.

Find a comfortable, quiet space where you can
clear your mind.

Because we don't have a problem. We don't
have a disorder. Or a deficit.

We have a difference.

And a difference is not a bad thing. In fact, some grown-ups might say that something 'made the difference', which means 'that was the right thing to do'.

Or 'we need to think differently' when they mean 'we are stuck'.

Or 'things are different now' when we could mean 'they got better'.

Because often the difference is just what people are looking for. Can you imagine if everyone on planet Earth thought exactly the same way? Our world would be sooo different and – if I'm honest – boring! This book could make the difference; it could help you think differently and, if yesterday was hard, show you ways to make tomorrow easier.

Our difference doesn't need to be a problem, but we all have a much easier, happier and better time when we understand it and have ways to explain how it can be the solution.

No one told me I had ADHD as a kid. People told me I was lazy (sometimes), that I was hyperactive (a lot) and didn't seem to see how that was confusing.

How can I be lazy *and* hyper? Surely I'm one or the other, right?!

Adults told me I couldn't concentrate, but also that I got too focused on certain things. That I spent too much time thinking or dreaming about one thing or the other.

So am I unfocused or too focused? Totally confusing!

I realized, when I found out I had ADHD, that people around me did not understand that I needed extra help sometimes, and that my brain worked differently. Some people with ADHD might take medications to help their brains, not because of other people, but because their brains do need help – and that's OK. It's like people with asthma may need an inhaler to help them breathe.

Before I was diagnosed with ADHD, others couldn't see a way to make me hyperactive about things that were good for me, for my job or for the world around me.

They couldn't understand how my focus could laser in on something that interested me, so they spent all their time trying to make me focus on something that I didn't like as much.

They couldn't see that what they called my *problem* was actually a *solution*.

Now, (sad truth alert!) the world isn't perfect. Some people will struggle to understand the different and fantastic ways in which your wonderful brain works. That is a fact, my friend. So sometimes you will need to find someone who can help you explain it, or do it yourself. But, if you can:

1. Understand how your brain works

2. Find an approach that works for you

3. Explain to that person why it works

4. Be ready to say *why don't we try it this way?*

YOU WILL HAVE THE SOLUTION.

You can be a leader.

Now I know that is a lot of responsibility, but responsibility is not a bad thing.

Being the penalty taker for Chelsea FC (a.k.a. my favourite football club!). Now *that's* responsibility. It's a responsibility that someone has been given because they have the ability (or power) to take penalties in a way other people can't.

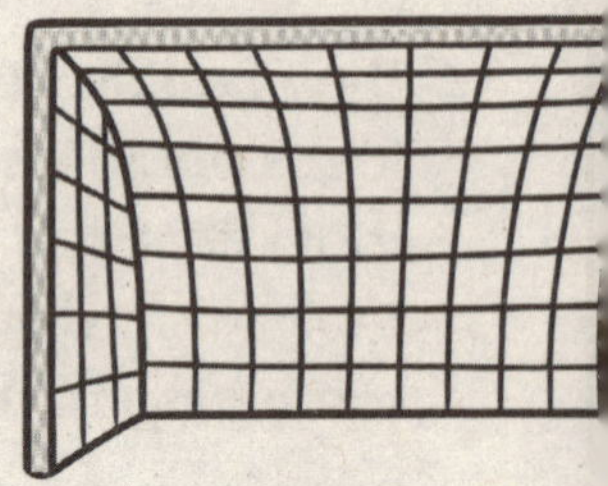

Being a doctor in a hospital. That's responsibility.

- **A firefighter.**

- **A caregiver.**

- **The Prime Minister.**

- **A singer in a band.**

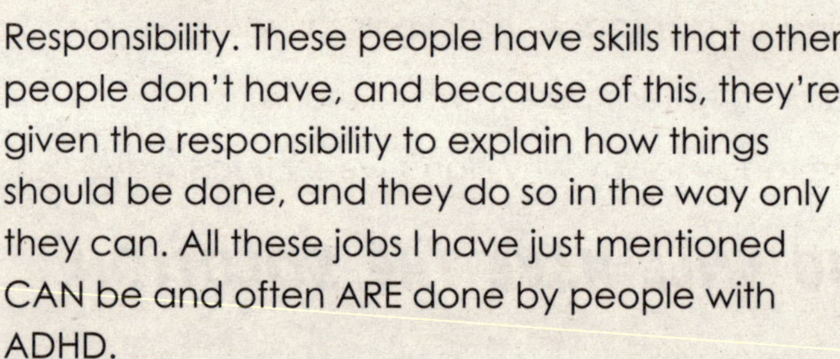

Responsibility. These people have skills that other people don't have, and because of this, they're given the responsibility to explain how things should be done, and they do so in the way only they can. All these jobs I have just mentioned CAN be and often ARE done by people with ADHD.

So don't let the fact that you might be different hold you back and stop you from doing anything.

Let's learn about how you are different,
and why that's a great thing.

Let's see how we can understand our
differences and how to make them work for us.

And let's get all the tools in our kit to help us
achieve our dreams.

Because that's how we do great things,
I promise!

CHAPTER 1

KNOWING YOURSELF, UNDERSTANDING YOUR POWER AND LEARNING HOW TO USE IT

The idea of this book is easy-peasy. We need to:

1. Know *who we are*:

   - What we like doing and what we want to achieve.

   - What we struggle with.

2. Learn *how to do those things well*:

   - What works for us and helps us achieve what we want.

   - What doesn't – and how to make the things we struggle with feel easier.

3. Understand how to *explain all of that*:

- Why we prefer to do things in our own special way.

- Why the *usual* ways might not suit us.

- Why some things may not go to plan, and the best way to get back on track.

Which sounds pretty simple, right?

Well, sort of. They *are* simple ideas, but they helped me realize some pretty big things.

You see, I only really started to wonder about who I was, what mattered to me and how I could be different *happily* after I found out I had ADHD. Before then, I was just trying to get by, often finding it hard, and ended up disappointed in myself and in other people who didn't understand me.

But it was by doing the hard work and thinking about simple questions like 'Who am I?' that I found life got easier. It was by starting with small questions, seeds that I planted in the ground, that I was able to grow.

To start with, I might have answered that question
– *Who am I?* – with a very short answer:

I'm me. Are we done now?

Well, again, sort of. But think about it, there are
other questions that come out of that, and each
answer is a chance to learn a little bit more. Try to
think of your answer to these questions as we go.

Where did I begin?

This is a chance to think about your parents, or the
people who care for you. (For me, it is my mum,
dad and big sister, Louise. Total legends!) They will
have an idea of who you are, what they wanted
for you on the day they first met you and looked
into your eyes.

Where am I now?

Maybe you are ten, eleven or twelve years old. You
have grown a lot from that day when you first
opened your eyes. The people around you have
watched you grow and learn. They have seen you
find things that make you feel happy, excited and
interested. They have watched you say, 'I don't
want to do that,' when you were asked (or told) to
do something that gave you that tough, mixed-up
feeling of frustration.

What can I do now that I could not do a few years ago?

Here you can see some things that *you* discovered, and *you* chose. No one has to tell you to do the things that you love, because you *want* to do them. That is important. If you can do those sorts of things in your life, as much as possible, you'll get bored way less and rarely get frustrated.

What is something that I don't like doing?

Sometimes it can feel like the things we *don't want to do* get way more attention from other people than the things we do. If, like me, you don't like doing maths homework, I'll bet you've spent more time talking (shouting, arguing?) about maths homework than whatever it is you like.

The things we *don't* like doing are as much a part of us as the things we do like. I had to spend time understanding and getting to know them, so I could find ways to make them easier and get them done – to make more time for the things I *did* like. And to find ways to make those tasks feel more like the things I enjoyed.

Here's an example. Let's stick with maths homework. If you are like I was, getting this done might take *hours*.

There's the **getting started** part. My parents would tell me to do it, I would make a random excuse and try to distract them, and then try to waste enough time with the hope that they would just say 'time for bed!'. This never worked. I would just end up starting way later, and have no time after I finished to do anything fun.

Then there was the stop-start. When I realized there was no point trying to avoid it any more, I would do a bit. Then I would get annoyed or bored and stop. I'd start singing a song to distract myself, look out of the window or pretend to go to the toilet.

I've tried *all* of these tricks. Believe me. And the problem was always the same. Soon I'd have to

start again and there would still be just as much maths homework to do.

Then there was the last phase. The hurry. *Uh-oh!* I'd realize it was getting late and it needed to get done. So I'd hurry through it at the last minute.

And what was the result? The hard thing, which I didn't like, ended up taking *more* time and feeling way *harder* than it needed to. It took hours when it could have been twenty minutes, and I could have spent that time gaming with my mates.

It was only once I got my diagnosis and learned that my brain was something I could manage that I thought about the next question:

Why would I spend so long doing (or trying not to do) things I didn't like?

Weren't there tricks and tactics, ways of helping my brain get hard things done quickly and well, which gave me time to do the things I *do* like?

This is where self-knowledge starts to become something we can climb to get a better view. If we can look at ourselves and the time we spend fighting with our maths homework, we can see other ways of doing things. I can put on some music, sit in a comfy, quiet space and set a timer.

Twenty minutes and we will be done.
Then we chill out and use the time to
do something fun. *Yeeeeaaaah!*

Because we can also think more
about what *we like* as a way to
make it easier to do things that
we don't.

You see, if you like sports but don't like
maths, then maybe you need to make maths
homework more like a sport. Maybe it can be
more like a competition or a race? If you like
music, maybe those maths questions could be
put to a song.

There are always ways to bring the things you like
into the things you don't. You just have to know
yourself and what works for you.

There are other great things about knowing 'who
we are'. It is always a good idea to take a bit of
time to try and build up your self-knowledge by
asking yourself questions. Knowing who you are
can be a powerful thing. Think of building your
self-knowledge like a garden orb-weaver spider
creating its famous web. From one strong thread
(the anchor), they make dozens of radial and spiral
threads that connect to form a single strong

structure. As Peter Parker knows, 'with great power comes great responsibility'. Well, I think it's worth asking yourself questions like:

Who do I want to be?

You are probably at an age when you see little kids and notice you can do things better or quicker than they can. Maybe you have looked at teenagers and grown-ups and realized that in just a few years, you will be like them too.

What kind of teenager do you want to be? What sort of adult would you like to become?

Because grown-ups always ask, 'What do you want to be when you grow up?' when, really, they mean, 'What job do you want to do?'

Now that can be a cool question – maybe you want to be a painter or a basketball player. Maybe you would like to be a teacher or nurse. It's good to think about that, but it's more important to think about *how you want to be* rather than *what you want to do.*

If you said you want to be a painter, really, you were saying *I want to be creative.*

I want to make something new in the world.

That's great, and it means you can do anything creative: paint, or write or design GIGANTIC buildings. Those things are all creative, and the part of you that makes you want to paint is the same part that will help you do all those other things.

Maybe you said you want to be a basketball player, which is totally cool. And it means lots of different things about *how you want to be*.

If you want to be a basketball player, you want to be active, fit and healthy, fast and strong. You want to be in a *team*.

That means working with other people, helping them and letting them support you too. If you decide to be those things, you can be a member of *any* team, and a fast, strong member of it.

Maybe you said you want to be a teacher or a nurse. This means you want to be *knowledgeable*, to be kind and care for people who need you.

All of those answers about *how you want to be* help you answer two important questions:

1. *Who am I?*

and

2. *What matters to me?*

TRY THIS

So write down **five things** that you are.
Good things only, please!

Here is my attempt:

1. I am a team player
2. I am creative
3. I am kind
4. I am funny
5. I am sporty

Keep a list of your best qualities somewhere you can see it. It reminds you what matters. You can revisit your list every few months to see what you can add. If you get really stuck, you could ask an adult you trust or a friend to tell you the things they value in you, and see if you agree.

✹ BEING KIND TO OURSELVES

My self-knowledge is a **big** part of the toolkit that made me start to feel awesome. Sometimes, it is also my shield. A hero does not only have to fight for their goals – they have to be able to defend themselves when others try to bring them down.

And sometimes we have to defend ourselves against ourselves.

Maybe you've been tempted to say mean things to yourself when things don't go to plan. Maybe you've said, 'I'm lazy', 'I'm naughty' or 'I just don't get it'.

But if you practise asking yourself, 'Who am I?' you can build a shield that protects you. You can see ways to change those hurtful comments into something more kind and more true.

Like when you say, 'I'm naughty', you probably mean 'sometimes I get frustrated'. And it is your self-knowledge that will help you choose the kinder, truer words.

'Naughty' is a **label** – which suggests it's something about us that doesn't really change – but 'sometimes I get frustrated' is just a feeling that everyone has, and feelings are things we can learn to change. I don't like labels like 'naughty', especially for kids and young people. I don't think it's right to label people. I think people can experience feelings that impact their behaviour, and their feelings can change.

Feelings can be emotions we experience **all** of the time, **some** of the time or **rarely**. If you think about *what* frustrates you, *how* you get through frustrating situations and *why* some things are worth working through, it's a way to understand yourself a little better and can make it easier to explain to yourself and other people why you are feeling frustrated.

If someone calls you 'lazy', it might be more accurate to say you concentrate in different ways to other people.

There are likely lots of things that make you feel *excited* and *focused*. Do you think you are lazy, in *any way*, when you are doing those things?

The answer is no. The things that give you the most energy are activities, games or lessons that make you REALLY happy. Maybe they involve other people, competitions or the chance to be creative. You need to learn from those things and find ways to fill everything you do with that sparky, fun energy.

You do things well. So please, please, please don't ever let anyone label you as lazy and don't ever say it about yourself. You think differently and it is a great thing if you can learn how to make the best parts of your difference show up in every part of your life.

ACTIVITY **1**
MY BRAIN'S SKILLS MAP

What?

A poster showing your strengths and challenges

Why?

To help us learn our strengths, challenges and ways to help

When?

Right now – for five minutes

How?

Start by writing what you think your brain does best (your strengths!). Draw a circle with your name in the middle. Then draw lines out to other circles where you write the things you do really well, like noticing little details about things, having a big imagination, caring about making things fair or helping others.

Now, in a different colour, draw some other circles. In these, write down the areas of your life where your brain might need some extra tools – things like remembering instructions, staying still, finishing long tasks. These are your 'challenges'.

Next, look at your strengths and your challenges together. Where could one of your strengths help you with one of the things on your challenges list? Draw an arrow going from your strengths towards the thing you need help with.

Maybe you put 'helping others' as a power and 'finishing long tasks' as a challenge. Maybe you could find a buddy, someone you have helped before, who can help you in return by reminding you where you are in a long task, and the steps you need to get to the end.

You will see that we all have powers and we all have areas where we need help. We just have to find ways to make our strengths support us with our challenges.

CHAPTER 2

KNOWING OURSELVES AND ADHD

So, I'm Sam, and it's nice to meet you.

I feel like we've been introduced to each other, and sort of also . . . been introduced to ourselves.

I think it is the start of a beautiful friendship.

We have tried to understand the **big picture** of ourselves, who we are, how we have grown

and where we want to go.
Now for the really interesting
part – getting to know who we
are in each moment.

*Huh, Sam? Are you saying I'm different people . . .
all the time?*

Well, we all change from moment to moment:
our energy, mood and feelings go up and down.
I know that I can feel like a completely different
person when I am having a sparky conversation
about something interesting, compared with
who I am when I'm doing something difficult that
I don't enjoy.

So we have to work out:

- How we are feeling.

- Why we are feeling like that.

- What it will take to feel good.

Because sometimes we can feel frustrated, bored
or angry. That is normal. Problems come when we
can't understand why. If we can understand why
we feel certain ways *and explain it*, then something
magical happens. Other people can help us, and
we can help ourselves.

I remember some of my saddest memories growing up were people saying, *'What is the matter with you?'* I might find something hard, get distracted or frustrated, and someone would say those words:

'What is the matter with you?'

I was sad because I didn't know what the matter was. I was even sadder because they didn't know either.

When really, nothing was the matter. I was different from them, but that didn't have to be a problem.

If I had known I was different, understood why and had figured out my best ways of working, there would have been no problem at all. I could have worked *with myself*, and I wouldn't have had to feel lonely because someone *couldn't understand me*.

I could understand myself. And I could explain myself – thank you very much.

So let's think about how we can understand ourselves even better. Let's add some tools to our kitbag that help us understand how we are feeling and help explain it.

Think of it like this:

- When someone drives a car, they use a speedometer to tell them how fast they are going. Without it, they might go too fast or too slow, because it can be hard to tell when they are in the moment.

- When someone is going out, they might check the weather forecast, so they can choose the right clothes or bring an umbrella.

- When grown-ups check their phones, there is a percentage showing the battery level, which helps them avoid it running out of charge.

In all parts of our lives, we use tools to see *how things are*, because they help us make better choices.

And you deserve some of the important tools. So here is one that I have found helpful for getting to know myself better.

ACTIVITY 2
ENERGY DETECTIVE JOURNAL

What?

A journal about your week

Why?

To learn about what gives you energy and focus

When?

One minute, a few times a day, for a week

How?

Over one week, write down when you feel super-focused, distracted or bored

Add what you were doing, where you were and who you were with, what you ate, when you went to bed. ANYTHING!

Afterwards, try asking: When do I work best? What helps me? What makes me feel good energy, and what makes me feel drained?

This is a super-cool activity and really helps me to understand what makes me feel good and what doesn't.

The Energy Detective Journal gives you
a sort of *speedometer* for your mind,
and a way to understand *your*
battery level. Even better, it tells
you about the things and places
that make you feel recharged and
those that make you feel drained.
Imagine if we all had torches but
didn't even know which batteries they
needed. Our torches would keep going dark,
and we'd be stumbling around all the time –
which is no good at all!

The tools that help us understand ourselves, our
energy levels, emotions and focus can all be
described as 'mindfulness'.

This does not mean your mind is full. Mindfulness
describes *ways to tell whether your mind is full.*
To make it feel calmer and emptied of rushing
thoughts. To understand what you are feeling,
why you are feeling it and how to make yourself
feel better.

Mindfulness is a speedometer, it's a battery check,
and it's a weather forecast. Every day, it helps us
move at the right speed, with the right amount of
energy and with the right clothes for the weather.

I like to think of mindfulness as a light I can shine on my mind and body to see how they are feeling.

Because feeling is a funny thing. If all we do is *feel*, it can be too much, and we can become overwhelmed. It is only when we can stop and look at our feelings that we see what created them and what they make us do.

It is only with mindfulness that we can get control of our feelings, rather than have our feelings control us.

Even better, it helps us *explain* how we are feeling and how the people, places and things around us could help to make us feel better.

So let's try a mindfulness task now.

ACTIVITY ③
PAUSE AND NOTICE (MINDFUL MOMENTS)

What?

A journal to track your energy and focus during the week

Why?

To help you understand what's happening inside you and what might help next.

When?

Right now and then once or twice a day

How?

Stop and ask yourself:

What's happening around me?

- Is it bright?

- Is it warm?

- Are there many people?

- What can I hear? See? Smell?

What's happening inside me?

- What can I feel in my body?

- Are there butterflies in my stomach?

- Can I feel the blood pumping in my veins?

What do I want to do next – and why?

- Do I want to run?

- Sit?

- Eat or drink?

- Be silent or talk?

In the future, you can write your answers down in a 'pause book'. This is a sort of diary, where you note down your feelings on different days. If you put this alongside your Energy Detective Journal, you will be able to see what makes you feel certain ways and learn how to make your day calmer.

If I'd had a pause book when I was a kid, I would have been able to explain that I climbed trees (which I did all the time) because it made me feel calm, not because I was being naughty. I would have been able to say that reaching up for the next branch, surrounded by fresh air and leaves, helped me relax.

I wasn't scrambling up them because I was hyperactive; it was because they made me feel *chilled*. Maybe the adults around me would have started *telling* me to go outside for some fresh air when I felt nervous and energetic, rather than *telling me off* for being hyper.

✸ THE RANGE OF OUR FEELINGS

We can't *improve* our feelings if we don't know what changes them. We have to know when we are feeling super-duper and what helped us get there if we are going to feel that way more often.

We all have a *range* of feelings and emotions. That's a big part of what makes us human. If we *only* had positive feelings, if we felt happy all of the time, things would actually be less interesting.

There would be no moody or angry songs, which can be kind of fun sometimes.

There would be no feeling of coming back from losing 2–0 down in the 80th minute to a 3–2 VICTORY! Honestly, being a football fan wouldn't be the same!

There wouldn't be a chance to be kind and cheer up your mates.

Our ups and our downs make life interesting, but they can make life painful if we don't understand why they happen. If we think it's just *luck* that makes us feel up one day and *luck* that makes us feel down, then we never really feel like we can make choices in our lives. We are just lucky, or unlucky.

But we can know about our moods and improve them. We can go from being 2–0 down to 3–2 up, and we can be the one who turns the match around. Guys:

WE CAN WIN!

I'd like to introduce you to a handy little way of thinking that I started doing when I was at school. I still find it sooo helpful, even now, when I'm feeling sad and upset about something and need to think about it differently to calm down. Give it a try!

✹ THE RULER METHOD

I bet you're thinking, 'What? I have one of those in my school bag!' Nope, I'm not talking about that kind of ruler! But I think it is even more helpful (sorry, teachers!). I'll give you a clue . . . each letter **(R-U-L-E-R)** is an instruction to help you. This stands for: **R**ecognize-**U**nderstand-**L**abel-**E**xpress-**R**egulate. I find it easier to write it all down and put it in a secret place, so I know I can find it and use it whenever I want.

We just have to learn to **(R)ecognize** our emotions and other people's.

This means saying things like: *'I'm feeling sad today,'* or *'Jane seems happy.'*

To **(U)nderstand** the *causes* of these emotions and the *effects* that they have.

'I'm feeling sad. I think it's because I'm disappointed about missing Pete's birthday because I was ill.'

Maybe the effect, or *result*, of feeling sad is that you aren't talking much to people in your class. Maybe you are even *avoiding* Pete.

That is an effect of your emotion, and it's not very helpful. If you are disappointed about missing Pete's birthday, it's probably because you would have enjoyed spending time with him and your friends.

So the effect – *not talking to Pete or your friends* – is actually leading to more of the thing that you were disappointed about.

If you can understand those causes, you might be able to avoid those effects. Because you've **(L)abelled** your emotion as 'disappointed', now you have a good word to describe it.

Instead of avoiding Pete, you can describe your feelings.

'Hey, Pete. I'm disappointed I missed your birthday because I was ill. It sounds like you guys had a really fun football party.'

You've **(E)xpressed** yourself. Pete knows that you care about him and like having fun with him, and now he has a chance to help you. Instead of avoiding him, you've given him a chance to invite you over to play football next weekend instead. It's true, being ill really sucks! But these things happen, and sometimes we have to rest so that we can get better quickly and get back to being our AWESOME selves.

Instead of being silent, sad and maybe even
angry at everyone else for having fun, you've
got a chance to have *more* fun. You've given Pete
the chance to be kind to you because you have
(R)egulated your emotions. That basically means
being the boss of your feelings. YOU can choose to
be excited that you have made a new plan with
your friends, and feel proud that you were honest
with your mate about feeling unwell. Good job!

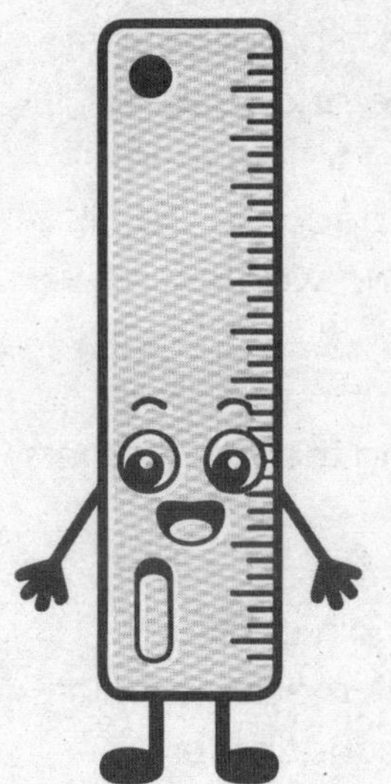

You've:

Recognized your emotions

Understood causes and effects

Labelled your emotions

Expressed them well

Regulated them

RULER.

When you experience big feelings that worry you, try
to think about the RULER. It is a way of making strong
feelings lead to good things, rather than something
that makes you feel bad or upset.

Strong feelings are not a bad thing. We *love* people with strong feelings. They're the best!

Think about a musician singing a deep, emotional song. No one thinks it is bad that the musician feels so strongly. It is *great* and brave that they have understood their feelings and then explained them through a song.

Think of your favourite sports star just scoring the winning goal. Do we think that it is a problem that they are running all over the place and shaking their hands in the air? No, we want to join them and share the strong feelings too because we all understand why they feel them and want to show them.

We love to get involved with strong feelings if others make space for us to join in.

So we have to help other people join us and understand our strong feelings. This means learning how to talk about feelings in ways that other people understand.

Back to Pete's birthday. We invited him into our strong feelings by telling him we were disappointed. We made him feel appreciated, and he appreciated us, then he helped.

But what if we had stayed silent? What would Pete have thought?

Sam didn't come to my birthday, and now he is ignoring me.

What would you think if you were Pete?

Sam is angry at me.

And anger is not a feeling that invites other people in. It can push them away. Anger is the opposite of an invitation, and for me, it is the opposite of a feeling. For me, anger is what happens when *we can't understand what we are feeling and it frustrates us . . .* Aarrgghh!

Anger is sadness dressed up in scary, spiky clothes.

It is what happens when we feel too confused to know that we are sad, or we feel frustrated about being sad, so we lash out.

Imagine that instead of telling Pete we were sad about missing his birthday, we bottle it up. We feel sad, and we go silent.

Then we see everyone else just continuing like everything is normal. In fact, for them it *is* normal. They don't know how we are feeling because we haven't told them. But we feel sad because no one has noticed how sad we are, and because we haven't explained, we get angry. We lash out to make them notice us.

Maybe we commit a bad tackle on Pete in the playground or shout, 'I didn't even want to go to your stupid party!'

We seem angry, but really we are sad and finding it hard to share.

That's why understanding our emotions and sharing them makes *such* a difference.

It's the difference between one story, where we talk to Pete and end up invited to his house next week to play, and another version where we are shouting at him and saying the *opposite* of what we are actually feeling.

So try using the RULER method to turn emotional situations into *good* situations, where your strong feelings are a sign that you care. When you do, your feelings can be a strength of you as a person because they make people feel cared about. How awesome is that?! It always makes me feel so much better.

✸ REWIND AND REWRITE

Maybe there will be a time when you forget to use the RULER trick. Don't worry, it can happen to any of us.

Maybe the whole situation plays out in the wrong way, and you end up shouting at Pete, showing anger instead of sadness, and hurting his feelings instead of making him feel appreciated.

What can we do?

Imagine you're writing a story, but you don't like what you've written. Do you have to stick with it anyway? No! You can just rewind and rewrite it. The same is true with real-life events. If something has gone wrong, spend a couple of minutes doing the next activity to explore how things could play out differently next time.

ACTIVITY 4
REWIND AND REWRITE

What?

Thinking about a tricky moment that has happened

Why?

To help us learn from tough moments and explain to people what we were really feeling

When?

After a tricky moment, an argument or a time we've been overwhelmed with emotion

How?

After that tricky moment, ask:

- What feelings did I show?

- What was I actually feeling?

- What made me feel that way?

- What did I do?

- What could I try next time to show my actual feelings?

You can share what you learned with someone else who experienced your tricky moment, so they can know what you were feeling and thinking.

Our ADHD gives us incredibly strong emotions, but in a way, we all have the power to rewind time (I mean, I always did want to be Doctor Who in his TARDIS! Or even better, Hermione Granger with her Time-Turner in *Harry Potter and the Prisoner of Azkaban!*). We all make mistakes, and sometimes we have BIG reactions and struggle to tell people how we are really feeling, but that doesn't mean we can't go back to the moment and explain what was actually going on. And trust me, other people always appreciate that.

But even better, we can also change the fuuuuuture (FUNKY SCI-FI MUSIC ALERT!).

OK, not like an *actual* time-traveller or wizard with a magic watch, but as a kid or grown-up who does things **now** to change what happens **next time**.

You see, Rewind and Rewrite lets us look back, learn and also explain what was *really* happening in hard moments.

But even better, we can use it to make hard moments happen less often in the future. If we know how we feel in those moments, we can set ourselves up with tools to make sure we are prepared . . . for the *best*.

✳ BEING PREPARED WITH SUPER-TOOLS AND SUPER-STRATEGIES

Everybody needs some top tools in their kit – tricks or tech that help them direct their powers. Maybe their super-suit stops them from stretching out of shape, or their glasses let them see around corners when they are moving at high speed.

Maybe they have an earpiece that gives them instructions for difficult moments. This is called 'strategy'.

A strategy is a plan designed to help us get what we want.

Sometimes you might use a strategy to win a playground game like Forty-Forty. You might make a plan after you realize you can run unseen past the recycling bins in the playground and make it to the home base. Thanks to your strategy, you win the game! Now you can put your feet up and chill!

Or in sports, if there are fast players in netball, football or rugby, teams might use a

'counter-attack strategy'. This means letting the other team come forward to attack, winning the ball and then using your speed to race up the other end before they can get back.

Or for me and the podcast I do with my friend Pete, we have to think of strategies that persuade new people to listen.

The good thing about a strategy, or plan, is that it helps us know what to do in difficult situations and saves us time thinking about the best option. A strategy might mean the difference between stopping and wondering about the next move and getting to where we need to be in time.

Strategies are tools that save us from using up time thinking. They tell us the right move to make, and usually we learn them because we have had to do something hard before.

So our strategies should be based on the information we have already collected about our behaviour and our feelings. Like a scientist, we can study our Brain's Skills Map to know what we're good at, our Energy Detective Journal to see what has made us feel a certain way, and when we are feeling strong emotions, we can whip out our RULER and help ourselves feel better.

So now we know a bit more about our behaviour and feelings, it's time to build our toolbox of things that can actually help us in the moment, and use our Rewind and Rewrite experiences to see what could have made situations work better.

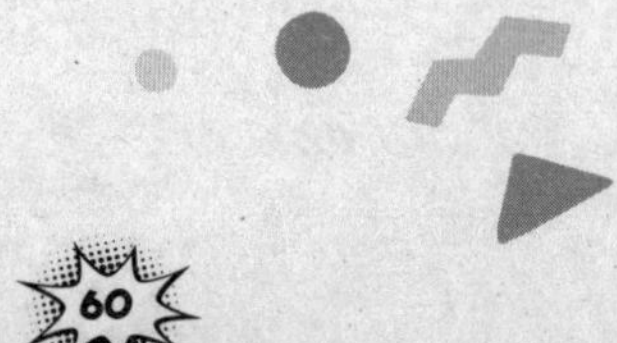

ACTIVITY 5
BUILD YOUR TOOLBOX

What?

Thinking about what will help you best

Why?

To give you strategies for emotional moments or energy changes

How?

Let's think about what we learned from other activities.

Did we learn about needing time to think about our emotions in the RULER method?

Or see how we can manage our energy levels by being an Energy Detective?

Maybe our last Rewind and Rewrite showed us that asking for help might have been the difference between making up and melting down.

Let's give ourselves the tools we can always carry to make our lives easier and improve our strategy.

For example, if you think *time* would be useful in a difficult moment, get a watch where you can set a one-minute timer. Explain to family, mates and teachers that this is something you use to pause and think.

Maybe your Energy Detective Journal showed that your fidget toy really helps you feel relaxed. Get one, show it to your teachers and explain that it is a tool. You can use it when you feel overwhelmed.

Or make small cards with phrases like 'I feel frustrated' or 'I need help', and keep them in your schoolbag. These can allow you to explain, quickly and quietly, how you feel. You might already be familiar with using an emotion wheel or emotion cards at school, but it's worth carrying them around and using them in other places, too.

Maybe it's creating playlists that you can listen to at home – one for when you want to get lots of energy and another for when you want to chillax (chill out, relax!). I have about ten different playlists . . . I'm not joking!

Your toolkit can be *anything* that helps. It all depends on your powers and what *you* want to do.

Spend time, like a scientist in a lab or a hero in their top-secret headquarters, studying *yourself*. Learn about your feelings, think about what you want to achieve and then create ways that help you get there.

When you do, you will realize that you have the power to do anything, as long as you can understand how, why and what it takes to do it.

CHAPTER 3

OUR HOME, OUR SPACES

For years, I lived right next door to my sister, Louise (a.k.a. one of my best mates!). And I used to just pop in and chat, wind her up as much as I liked, and then make her do funny Instagram and TikTok videos with me. Sounds great, right?

My home is very important to me, and the way it *feels* makes all the difference. If you don't think I'm serious, then hear this: when I designed my house, I said two things.

1. I want my kitchen to feel like a cold glass of fizzy water with a slice of lemon.

2. I want my bedroom and sitting room to feel like a hot cup of tea.

Feelings

Maybe you understand exactly what I mean straight away, or maybe it needs some explaining.

That's the thing about being unique; sometimes we understand and describe the world differently from other people. Some people get it; others need a bit more time, and that's fine.

What I mean when I say my kitchen should be like a cold glass of fizzy water is this: I want it to be *fresh and refreshing*. This means it is clean, it feels bubbly and sparkling: a place that gives me energy.
I want to step into it, drink it all in and go *ahhh*, just like you do after a big sip of a cold, fizzy drink!

I want my kitchen to be a great place to be on a hot day, with nothing fuzzy or sticky: just cool, clear and peaceful.

When I say I want my bedroom and sitting room to be like a hot cup of tea, I mean relaxing. I want them to feel soft and cosy (just like the fur of my two super-cute ragdoll cats – the *furrrrriest* cats in the world! Their names are Albus and Cedric, because I absolutely LOVE Harry Potter, and they are two of my favourite characters!). I want it to be the best place to be on a cold evening: somewhere safe and comforting. I want it to feel like the best hug ever.

I bet you can understand that, because when we describe our feelings properly, people usually do.

I also think you might, because we *all* feel different in different spaces.

Think about how you feel at a swimming pool, and then in a nice warm cafe. The two places create very different thoughts and feelings. At the pool, you might feel a sort of cool energy, ready to dive right in or go down the epic water slide, but later, when you are all dried off and probably quite hungry (I am always hungry after swimming!), you might crave the warmth of a cosy cafe with a hot chocolate!

Thinking about the spaces where we spend our time and how they make us feel is just another way of understanding ourselves and what gives us power.

You do not want to sit beside a warm log fire under a blanket before you go and do a 100-metre race, do you? Of course not! You want to feel energized and ready to be your speediest self.

If we can understand our spaces, we can use them like our toolkit, as ways to send our minds in the right direction and get our powers working for us.

So let's put our detective hat back on (maybe a detective coat as well . . . they always seem to wear a particular coat!) and instead of just detecting energy, let's be a Space Detective, too.

ACTIVITY 6
SPACE DETECTIVE

What?

Thinking about how you use rooms and spaces around you for different activities

Why?

To help us understand the places where we spend a lot of time, and how they make us feel

How?

By investigating the places where we spend time and seeing how we feel

Day 1

Go to the main spaces in your house and write them down:

- Kitchen
- Sitting room
- Bedroom
- Bathroom
- Garden / balcony (if you have one)

Then, sit in each of them and think about
how you feel:

- **Notice what your heartbeat is like
  (is it really fast, or slow?)**

- **Whether it is bright or quite dark
  in there**

- **What sounds there are**

- **Whether you can concentrate or
  if you feel distracted**

Write down what you find.

Day 2

Go back to the spaces in your home. Now try to
do something in them – homework, drawing or
quiet reading are good ideas.

Write down how focused you feel and some
notes, such as:

- **I feel distracted in the kitchen because
  there is a lot going on.**

- **I like that I can play quiet music in my room
  when I read.**

- **The sitting room carpet feels good against
  my feet.**

At the end, think about what makes one space good for focus and another not so good.

Make a list of things that help you focus and things that don't, like this:

Things that help me	Things that DON'T help me
Quiet spaces	Changing noises
My own music	Cold
Warmth	High stools
Nice-feeling carpets	Bright light
Low light	Different smells

Now you know the sort of spaces that help you relax and focus. They are warm, quiet and comfortable, with dim light and nice-feeling carpets.

That sounds *pretttttty* good to me as well!

The fun thing about being a Space Detective isn't really the research; it's *making* the space that works for you afterwards. Once you have got all the information about the type of space that fits snuggly around your mind, it's time to try and create it.

This is not a big job, but it is an important one. Think about a superhero and their life as an example. In comics and films, lots of their stories take place in busy, exciting places: on top of tall buildings, racing after fast cars and standing up to baddies in basements and lairs.

But there is another place where we usually see them: their safe space, the place where they can be calm.

Because a superhero can *never* be super all the time. A power cannot stay powerful if it is always being used. Heroes have to plug themselves in and recharge, just like a tablet or a phone. So they create a calm corner of their world where they can be themselves. Still super, just a little bit more quietly.

You deserve that kind of space, too. Your mind is probably quite fast and powerful, rushing around from one idea to the next, thinking about other people and how to help them, or about the things that make you excited.

But that is tiring. It is only possible to go that fast if you also have a break. Slow down. Take time. So let's think about what your space, your secret cave or calm corner looks and feels like. Let's try and make it.

✸ YOUR CALM (AS A CUCUMBER!) CORNER

OK. This is kind of cool, and if you have never had a chance to make a space your own before, then I'm totally excited for you. I told you about how I designed my own house, and trust me, it was AMAZING – sort of like feeling your thoughts fly out of your brain into the world and become a room!

It doesn't have to be hard work; it doesn't have to use up all of your pocket money and it doesn't even need *new things*. Your calm corner is the place where you bring together the things that help you recharge and focus.

Let's use the example I had (which is exactly the kind of space I love) to show how you can turn detective work into results. I like somewhere that:

- is quiet

- has my music

- is warm

- has nice-feeling carpets

- has low light

I'll add in a couple of extra things too:

- a fidget spinner

- headphones

- some plants (maybe a cactus? No, I'll go with a nice leafy one!)

- good cushions

OK, so let's go: how do we make this space?

Well, it should be quiet. How does our room sound? If there is a lot of noise from outside, we have to work around it – we can't make our family stop what they're doing. So we will get our headphones. OK: check!

We like it warm. OK. Where are we going to set up our calm corner? Let's put it near the radiator.

Like it warmer? OK, let's find a favourite blanket in the house and put it right there. It can go across your lap when you are in your calm corner, studying or chilling.

Carpets. What does the floor feel like in our room? Is it the right kind of feeling for a calm corner? If it is, then *great*; but if it isn't, let's get some help.

Try and think about your *favourite* feeling against your feet. Maybe it's a rug that's in your house. Ask one of the adults if you can put it in your calm corner. If you can't, think about another one that you can.

If you can't find one, then here's a great solution: socks. Find your comfiest pair of socks and put them in your calm corner. They can be like a blanket for your feet. So instead of putting your feet on a rug, you can put a rug *around your feet*. Toasty!

Think about the lights in your room. I like to make the light soft when I'm trying to concentrate super-hard on something. Bright lights above my head can feel a bit too much when I need to calm down. So take a look at the lamps in your house. Get someone a little taller and more grown up to help you with this!

Lights are all *different*. They all create different sorts of light: some will be sort of orange, others will be pure bright white. Think about which one feels the most *calm-cornery*.

Ask if you can put the most suitable one in your room. If not, then see if you can create a similar light feeling with help from your grown-ups. This might mean buying something, but it doesn't need to cost loads of money. Maybe a few fairy lights will do it, or maybe you need a new lampshade for a light you already have.

Time to get creative! Try lights in different places
(maybe some under your bed for a warm spaceship
glow), or at different heights to make it feel like sunset,
or in different colours.

Ask your parents or carers to be honest with you about
what can be done.

Finally, favourite cushions. Oh yes! You must have
some that feel extra squishy – hug 'em and squeeze
'em good. I know I do. So get them in your calm
corner too.

Now, sit there and relax.

Give that fidget spinner a nice, slow spin.

It should be like a warm hug for your mind.

Remember, you want your calm corner to be
somewhere to do homework or read, too, so think
about adding a surface to work on. This could be a
desk, but there are also simpler ways if that takes up
too much space or costs too much money. You could
get a lap desk, which could work. Or maybe a super-
simple small table you can cover with a nice fabric.

This is all about exploring what works for you. So get
creative. I promise that after a few days, you'll start to
love your calm corner. It will be somewhere you can

focus and get things done (quickly, making time for the fun stuff), or relax and think. Like everyone, you'll start to find that the hard stuff you do outside gets easier when you have a place to prepare, repair and maybe even just . . . *umm* . . . stare? (Hey, I wanted to rhyme!)

This is because the places where you spend time can change how you feel. Your room is a place where you live, and so is your mind, so think about how the two can help each other. That has been really great for me and always makes me feel so calm.

There are a lot of things in the world that I can't control: noisy rubbish collections outside my bedroom, rain clouds and how my football team performs, but I try to think about the things I can. Your calm corner is a place where you are the hero, and you can be in control. We've got this!

✸ FEELINGS MESSAGE BOARD

We can go one step further when thinking about our mind as another place where we live. We can make our calm corner a place where the feelings we have inside come out into the world. We can create a Feelings Message Board!

The message board is another tool – another speedometer for our brain – which lets us take our feelings and turn them into something we can see and share more easily. You know how sometimes you don't even realize you are hungry until someone takes a big pasta bake out of the oven, or don't realize you are tired until you see your bed?

Well, sometimes we need to see things to know how we are feeling.

So the message board is a mini-whiteboard, or blackboard (or really any colour board you choose!) that lets us put our feelings outside our brains, so we can see them and get to know them better. It also (and trust me, this is important) helps us to remember things we need to do. It makes you feel good about yourself, which is NEVER a bad thing.

ACTIVITY 7
FEELINGS MESSAGE BOARD

What?

A small board in our calm corner where we post messages using simple sentence starters

Why?

To remind us to check our feelings, and to make them something we can see

How?

Pick a few simple sentence starters and write them on the board. Or if you love art (like me!), then draw some pictures of what you want to say. They can be anything you like, but try to pick some that help you check your feelings, some that help you remember things you might forget (oh hello, PE kit . . . where have you been?) and others that make you feel thankful for nice things in your life.

Here are some examples:

- Today I feel . . .
- Today I want to . . .
- I should remember to . . .

- I might need help with . . .
- I feel happy that . . .
- Today I . . .
- Tomorrow I . . .

TOP TIP

These last three are great to do at the end of the day.

When you take a moment to say, 'I feel happy that . . .', you can remember something good about your day, or something in your life that makes you feel lucky: a warm bed, a sunny day or a nice dinner.

When you fill in 'Today I . . .', you have a chance to mention something you feel proud of – to pat yourself on the back for working hard at something, being kind or doing well.

When you complete 'Tomorrow I . . .' you have a chance to start getting ready for another great day (*Tomorrow I will take over the worrrrrld!*). This way, when you're sleeping, your body will already be building itself up to a great day. It might also be a good place to put reminders for things you need (oh, history homework . . . you're still here . . . I forgot about you!).

Your Feelings Message Board can be something completely private. Just like your calm corner or your secret hero cave, it can be yours only, or you can share it with your family. Maybe it would help you to know how *they* are feeling, too. If that's true, put it up on the fridge, and everyone can add their thoughts and feelings.

But it's fine if you want to keep this tool for yourself. It's great, and for me it's important because it keeps me thinking about my *mini-wins*.

Mini-wins are the little things that have gone well, small moments where I have made an effort. **If you think of a superhero, it's not just the big, giant, saving-the-world moments that feel great – the small ones do, too.**

It's helping the cat down from the tree, or the elderly lady crossing the street. I love to make people smile and laugh – it's my favourite thing in the world! These are mini-wins, and the more you can remember each of them, the more you'll realize what a winner you are.

I fed the cat.

That is a mini-win (don't just ask me, ask the cat . . . 'MEOWW!').

I remembered Ellie's birthday.

WIN.

I filled in my Feelings Message Board.

WINNER, WINNER, CHICKEN DINNER!

I helped put out the plates for THE chicken dinner.

Win.

The super, stupendous, splendiferous thing (sorry, dude – long words there . . . I wanted to sound smart! They mean 'amazing' and 'wonderful') about writing down our mini-wins is that it makes us more likely to keep on winning. I mean it – lots of scientists have studied it, and the feeling you get from mentioning your mini-win pushes you towards more wins in the future.

Think of your mind like a garden.

If you try and ride your bike across long grass, you might have to push and pedal hard to get to the other side.

But if you cycle across it a few times, there will be a little path where you have cycled before – a line through the mud where everything is pushed down and easier to go across.

The more times you do that, the flatter the path will be and the easier it will be to cycle across it. Each time you have a mini-win, you make that path easier to ride, and the more you note it down, the more you will remember the way towards it. Problem solved!

Once again, like that time-travelling wizard or Chronogirl with the magic watch, you can change the future by remembering something from the past, in your present moment.

OH, THE POWER! 

CHAPTER 4

THE PEOPLE WE SHARE OUR HOME WITH

All of the tools I talk about work in similar ways. They all improve our present moment and make it more likely that in the future, things will go better too.

Thinking about our feelings using our old buddy, the **RULER** (remember that from earlier? **R**ecognize, **U**nderstand, **L**abel, **E**xpress, **R**egulate), means that the next time strong feelings come up, it will be easier to work with them.

Using the Rewind and Rewrite method after emotional situations go wrong makes it more likely that we won't need to rewind in the future.

Celebrating mini-wins makes us more likely to win tomorrow.

It's the same if we think about happier ways to live with our families at home. You see, we've spoken about how we make our minds and our rooms

comfy, but another important thing in any house is how comfortable our relationships are.

Do you feel like your family understands your feelings? Or that you have ways to ask them for help when you need it? Are there ways to make those difficult conversations feel easier after things go wrong?

It's OK if you answered no to any of these questions. Most people don't have all the answers when it comes to relationships, but the great thing is that there are tools to help us work on them. Even better, once we start using these tools, they make our conversations clearer, and it feels easier to have them in the future.

MAGIC.

But actually, it's not. It's just another type of strategy or plan. Just like a sports team has a strategy to make it easier to play their game, strategies for speaking to the people we live with make life easier and simpler.

Now, maybe you are one of the *very rare people* who don't like things to be easy and simple. You like them hard, complicated and painful. *Ermm . . .* wow! Well, you do you!

If you are one of those people, this section might not be for you.

But if you are part of my crew that likes things to be easy and simple (and trust me, you're my people if you do . . .), then let's get together and 'ave a *good ol'* chat about how to have good new chats.

Because the way we speak to people makes all the difference.

'GIMME THAT PENCIL!!'

Hearing this would probably make you feel quite different to someone politely asking, 'Could you pass the pencil, please?'

I think people sometimes make politeness seem quite strange. Like it's some old-fashioned rule created by Victorians, when really it's just a way of speaking that makes your needs clear and helps others feel appreciated.

This is not a chat about politeness, but it's similar. You see, the way we speak to each other can make all the difference. If we can find ways to speak truthfully and kindly, with an effort to be honest about how we feel, then our conversations can be pretty sweet.

If we try to hide how we feel, demand things or let our emotions do the talking, then normal chats can become arguments, and we don't want that . . . no, sir!

I think about arguments in the same way that I think about maths homework taking two hours instead of twenty minutes: A. Waste. Of. Time. 

Now, I'm not saying we shouldn't feel strong emotions or tell people how we feel.

It's OK to disagree, speak up or argue *for* what is right.

The problem is when we don't say what we mean, and end up saying things that are mean instead. Then feel guilty. Then apologize. But often *still* leave feeling a bit guilty.

We can save a whole lotta time and sadness if we can find ways to say what we really mean, in ways that make people understand what we're feeling.

The good thing is you're probably an expert in understanding how you feel now. You've used the RULER method, you've created a Feelings Message Board and you've got a feelings toolbox that's growing sooo big, you might have to move it to the shed!

You are the expert. Well done, you!

So now is a great time for
you to help the people
you live with improve
their communication.

Yes sir/ma'am. Today,
you are the teacher.

⭐ HELPING OUR FAMILY

It's time for you to take the lead and show your
family what good communication is all about. Just
because people are older, it doesn't mean they
always know the best way to talk about their feelings,
to apologize after falling out with someone or how to
have the healthiest and happiest days they can. Trust
me: I'm a grown-up, and I'm still learning!

So now we are going to chat about three different
activities that you can get everyone in your house
to do, to make life feel a little super-er.

ACTIVITY 8
TALK TIME

What?

Cards with topics to talk about in a group of people you trust

Why?

To help everyone with each other's thoughts, feelings and efforts

When?

Before or after dinner, when everyone is together

How?

Get pieces of card (cutting them out together can be a great way to start). You should each have five.

On one card, each write: **'Celebration'**

Then start with something like:
A small win I had / Someone who was kind to me / One thing I'm proud of / One thing I'm grateful for

On the next card, each write: **'Challenges and Coping'**

Think about:
*A moment today when I could have used more
help / Something that frustrated me, but I stayed
in control / A problem I solved in my own way /
One thing I want to try again tomorrow . . .*

On the next, write: **'Feelings and Connection'**

Think about:
*A feeling I noticed today / Something I noticed
about someone at the table / A moment I felt
understood / A moment I felt misunderstood . . .*

On the next, write: **'Looking Ahead'**

Some sentence starters to help you:
*Tomorrow I will / A habit I'm working on is /
One thing I want to understand better is /
The next skill I will learn is . . .*

And on the last one: **'Group Thoughts'**

Add a sentence starter like:
*Something we all did well together / A challenge
we faced together / Something we can try together
this week / A moment when we could have
supported each other more . . .*

Then, when everyone has finished writing, put your
cards face down, and each have a go at turning one
over, and then all give your own answer.

By the end of this activity, you should each have
five new cards, but you can do more if you find
them useful. They are great for making us notice
things we might miss, moments when we could
have helped each other or small, kind things that
we have been doing.

Even better, they remind us to make more
effort each day, because we might think 'that's
exactly the sort of thing I would like to mention at
Talk Time . . . this is a good moment to try and
practise that new skill.'

Because we are often zooming around – up and
out of the house to school, out to play, in for dinner
or to get ready for bed – sometimes the things
which really matter, like talking to each other about
how we feel or about what we would like to
change, get pushed to the side. We are so busy
hurrying around that we don't take time to work on
making things better.

It's practice. For life. And we all know practice
helps us improve. And it's no use just practising the
things we are already good at or enjoy, either. We
have to work on the hard stuff, too.

If we only ever made up funny songs in music
lessons, we wouldn't learn things like scales or get
better at the difficult jumps between certain notes.

When we slow everything down and focus on what is difficult and what we want to improve, then we can make a difference. And that is true for life at home.

✷ RULES

There is another part of home life that sometimes causes a bit of argy-bargy, or a few arguments or debates.

Rules.

Rules caused me a lot of problems growing up. They seemed to be EVERYWHERE, and no one seemed to explain *why* they were there. Like 'Manners' or 'Politeness', they felt like they had been passed down in some dusty old book that the grown-ups could read, but I was never shown.

I was told they existed for good reasons, but no one really took the time to explain *why they were useful.*

'Those are the rules.'

'That's just how it is.'

'It has always been done that way.'

These were answers I heard *every* day. And those kinds of answers really annoy me.

Because I don't mind rules, if I know *why they exist.*

If I know they make sense, that they are useful and that everyone respects them (adults and kids, teachers and students, heroes and villains . . . OK, maybe not the villains, as their whole thing is breaking rules, isn't it?!). I *genuinely* have no problem following rules. If they make sense, are useful and everyone respects them, I don't mind following them.

For me, understanding *why* is often the really interesting part of anything. A fact like 'it takes light eight minutes to reach the Earth from the Sun' is cool, but it is the *why* that interests me.

It's because the Sun is 150 MILLION kilometres away (that's the average journey to school, 40 MILLION TIMES!!).

And light travels at 300,000 km per second. Just to be clear, that's pretty fast. A human can run up to about 12.4 metres per second, so that light is about 25 MILLION TIMES FASTER THAN USAIN BOLT. (He's the guy that holds the world record for the 100-metre sprint, by the way!)

This is a long way of saying that understanding *why* is much more interesting than just knowing *what*.

And rules are much less frustrating and much more useful if we understand *why* they exist. They are even better when we can be involved in creating them and give our own reasons for *why* they should be followed. When we do this, we move from 'Rules' (where you think of a strict old teacher in a dusty suit) to 'Agreements' (which is something we come up with together).

So how do we move from *rules* to *agreements*?

ACTIVITY 9
TEAM AGREEMENTS

What?

An activity that helps us decide on the best agreements to start with

Why?

Because, unlike rules, agreements are something we help create, we own and we understand

When?

Whenever everyone who lives in the house is together and in a good mood

How?

Warm up by each saying some things you *like* about your family – things you all do without even thinking about it that much. These could be anything, but what you might find is that certain things have been agreed on, like:

- We always make an effort to surprise someone on their birthday.

- We try to say I love you before we leave the house.

- We don't go to bed without making up after an argument.

Then you can agree on some ways to act when you make your agreements.

- All ideas are welcome.

- We don't judge each other.

- Every member of the team can share their thoughts and is listened to.

Then you can start creating. Each person can suggest one agreement for each of these categories:

Communication and Emotion

- We try to use a kind voice first, even when we are frustrated.

Helping Each Other

- We fix problems together.

- We remind each other kindly, not in a mean way.

Routines

- *Everyone* takes part in a five-minute cleaning time after dinner and before bed.

- We all check the calendar together each morning so we know what is happening that day.

Relationships

- We celebrate effort, no matter if we win or lose, get something right or wrong.

- We accept people's apologies.

Self-Management and Respect

- We let each other finish what we're saying.

These are all great agreements. Once you have all the suggested agreements, discuss and vote on one favourite agreement for each category.

See how it goes.

If you like having agreements, maybe you'll start coming up with more. Soon you might have thousands! (But that might be too much . . .)

I wish I had had more agreements, conversations and fewer rules when I was a kid.

I got in a lot of trouble for asking 'why?'; for trying to understand the reasons behind rules, and now I see that it could have been avoided.

Because it must be difficult for grown-ups like teachers, sports coaches and parents to hear a kid say 'Why?' when they tell them to do something. They are trying to get something done, and it feels like the kid who is asking why is saying, 'I don't agree' or 'That's a silly idea'.

But for me, I *really* wanted to understand why something was happening. I wanted to know why a rule helped everyone learn better, or why a coach made a decision about a sports team we were on. Learning why is a big part of understanding, but we have to be clever about how we use the word 'why'.

Here's an example from my life.

When I was fifteen, my football coach told me I was out of the team and not starting the next match.

I was really disappointed, but I bet I just
looked angry, and asked, 'Why?!'

So he replied, 'Because I said so.'

End of story.

I think I stormed out of the changing
room and slammed the door. I was angry.

Now, let's Rewind and Rewrite that situation for my
coach and me.

Let's begin with *how* he could have let me know.
By thinking about my feelings, he could have
realized it would be disappointing and tried to
explain straight away.

Coach: 'Sam, we're going to give John a go up front
this week. He has been making a great effort in
training, and I want to have a few different options in
that position.'

That would be a great start, and the coach could
have saved us all some trouble if he had explained it
that way. I wouldn't have needed to ask why,
because I already knew. John was working hard and
deserved a go, and it would be good for the team if
we understood how to play in different ways.

I might not have been happy, but I would have understood *why*.

Now imagine the coach didn't do that, and instead he said:

Coach: 'Sam, you're out; John, you're in.'

How could I respond in a way that expressed my real feelings and disappointment, and also find out the reasons why?

Well, ideally, I could take a moment to think about it. I would possibly understand myself and express myself better if I waited until the end of the team meeting.

One reason grown-ups sometimes say things like 'Because I said so' is that they are busy making sure lots of other people are seen and listened to, and they try to close down the conversation we are trying to have. It doesn't mean that they don't care about you, though!

I bet the coach wouldn't say 'Because I said so' if I asked him later, after training, when he didn't have to speak to a whole big group.

So I could ask him later. What could I say?

How about:

Sam: 'Do you mind explaining why I'm not in the team next week, Coach?'

That's better, and more likely to get a useful answer.

But I could probably do even better by thinking about what I really want. My real goal was to understand why I was out *and what I had to do to get back in.*

I wanted to be in the team, so I had to understand what I needed to do. So I could have said at the end of the session:

Sam: 'Coach, I understand why you are giving John a go, but I really want to get back into the team. Could you let me know what you want to see me work on, in training and in matches?'

Now the coach is probably going to rub his eyes and gasp, wondering what has happened to the old Sam who just said 'Why?!' and then had an argument. Once he has come back down to earth, he is more likely to think that the new Sam is really thoughtful, and that is just what we need in this team.

Then he could give me the information I needed: work on crossing, try harder to tackle defenders and try and get fitter because we have a lot of matches coming up. Useful information that I would not have got if I just asked, 'Why?!'

What you can see here is that this is much more like an agreement than a rule. I worked with the coach to understand what we both needed and helped each other to get it. The coach needed to try some different things with the team, needed me to get better at crossing, and needed to be able to explain his decisions in a quiet moment without everyone watching.

I needed to be told why I was not in the team and what I could do to get back in.

We are in agreement – and agreement makes the world go round!

It is by agreeing that we find ways to reach our goals that don't feel like effort or rules. It's where what we want lines up with what other people want, and we all help each other get there.

And that is definitely true at *school*.

CHAPTER 5

SCHOOL

There were lots of things I loved about school, but not many of them involved lessons. I just couldn't understand why everything seemed to involve sitting in silence. I like moving around, talking and learning through conversations, so the lessons didn't work very well for me.

It also seemed like we were trying to learn *how* to sit and work quietly, as if it were a skill I would need for the rest of my life.

I had three main hopes and dreams at that time, and none of them involved sitting in silence once I left school.

I would either be:

1. a footballer (sort of obvious, I know, but I *loved it*)

2. a climber (I will explain more about that in
a minute!)

3. Indiana Jones (a super-cool archaeologist film
character, who isn't afraid of danger or fighting
villains!)

(Not Indiana Jones *exactly*. I wasn't going to take
the place of the guy in the films, but I was planning
to travel the world, discovering artefacts and
monuments and generally being a *super*
archaeologist.)

From as early as I can remember, archaeology and
ancient history interested me. It's like a puzzle, or a
jigsaw, where we only have a few pieces and have
to put them together to see a whole other world.
That world may be a few thousand years ago, and
it is one discovery, one pot or jewel that will unlock
its secrets – and that really excites my brain.

It is important to notice the *kinds* of things we find
interesting and what they have in common. This
can help us find new, similar interests, and it can
also show us the ways of learning we find fun –
which we can then use to make harder things
easier, or more interesting.

Take my brain. These are things that make it
interested:

Gamification: *Can this activity, task or job be described as a game?*

For archaeologists, this is easy: you are an explorer. *Travel around the map and find artefacts. The older or more valuable the artefact the more points you score.*

Football . . . well, that's *already a game,* and climbing sort of is too.

Imagination/Creativity: *Is it helpful to think differently?*

I find it hard to be interested in things where there is only one right way to do them.

My attention always goes to activities where we can think differently, from a different direction or even suggest whole new wild ways of thinking to unlock the answers. As a kid I absolutely loved Lego, where I could problem solve and figure out creative ways to make a new model.

If an activity can be made to look like a game, requires some creative thinking or involves movement, then I get super-interested and focused. I think I knew that as a kid, but I didn't completely understand it.

I knew it, clearly, because I wanted to do jobs when I grew up that involved all of those things. Football is obviously a creative game where we move a lot, and archaeology we have seen can be too, but what about climbing?

Well, the funny thing about climbing is that it wasn't a job really when I was growing up. When I was a kid in the 1990s (many THOUSANDS of years ago), rock climbing wasn't that popular, so people weren't really sure what I meant when I said I wanted to be a climber.

I was sure, though. I meant that I
wanted to climb things.

All day.

Every day!

Tall things, really tall things and sometimes even
mega-tall things – if people needed them climbed,
they could call me.

Apparently, that wasn't a job, but it's definitely a
skill in some jobs.

Tree surgeons climb up trees all the time to cut
down old branches and make space for new baby
ones. There's mountain rescue, which also involves
a lot of climbing, and scaffolders definitely climb on
building sites.

You can't say that these jobs are *just* climbing, but
you also can't say they *aren't* climbing.

And climbing makes me feel SO GOOD. When I
climb, everything in my mind switches off, apart
from the part that is focusing on my balance and
the next branch. It's sort of like I'm not Sam, the guy
with a body in the tree; I *am* just the bit that is
climbing. I am the movement.

Like if climbing was a thing, it's me – and there is
nothing else except the climbing (is it just me or has
the word climbing started to look really weird?
Like . . . where did that b in the middle come from?
Clime-BING?!).

OK, that's all a bit out there, but I'm sure you have
felt something similar when you are really focused
on something you love. It becomes all there is.

So . . . where was I? Oh yes, school. Sometimes my
brain goes off on a random little thought (do you
get that too?) and ends up thinking about things
like the weird B in the middle of the word clim**b**ing
(bing!), when I am supposed to be talking about
school, but that's fine!

In fact, depending on where we are and what we
are doing, it can be a good thing. I host a podcast,
and people like it when I go off and talk about
random things.

I was also in the jungle on the TV
series *I'm a Celebrity . . . Get Me
Out of Here!* and told people
long stories about things I found
interesting, going off in loads of
different directions, and my
campmates loved it.

I have realized as I grow older that my ability to let my mind wander in the most interesting direction is a power as well as a challenge, even though I was mostly told it was a problem at school.

Because at school we are asked to keep our minds on just one thing for long periods and stay still while we do it. You can see how that was difficult for me, and you too, I bet! As I said, I appreciate movement, creativity and gamification, so unless I could find ways to bring those into my classes, I would often lose interest.

And you might not think there are many ways for an energetic, creative kid who likes to think about lots of different things to succeed in quiet classrooms, but there are. In fact, those are just the things that we are going to discuss today.

But before we do, let me say one more thing.

REMEMBER:

It's possible that some of your skills will be appreciated much more outside of school than in it. Like I said, I have a whole job based on being a creative, energetic, rambling-on-tangents kind of guy, but I had to wait until I had left school to really see those skills get valued.

That might be true for you as well, and while I hope it isn't, you should remember that your whole life won't always be like school. The curriculum is also there to help us learn key knowledge and skills across all subjects. There will be a time and a place where energy is a valuable thing, and being able to think in different creative ways is too, and lots of tree-climbers are required in life!

Or perhaps you are quieter. You may be so busy trying to fit in, or trying to please everyone, or simply daydreaming, that you stay really quiet most of the time. Maybe you don't speak up and share your struggles, and don't feel confident to let your powers shine! This can be just as challenging to handle as being told to sit still when you're feeling fizzy (excited and energized).

But **VERY IMPORTANT INFORMATION HERE . . .** people who want to be teachers and choose to work in schools do so because they really care about you and want to help you do great things. They really do! All of us learn in different ways and have different things that we are good at or find hard. Teachers love to know how you learn best and will make time to speak to you and your grown-ups to think of new ways that you can really enjoy learning, and make time for you to tell them

what you find hard to do, too. Some schools might even make your own special learning plan to help . . . how cool is that?!

One of your teachers' main jobs is to give you the tools you need for secondary school and the important exams you'll take when you're a bit older. That's why you, your teachers and your grown-ups need to work together to find a way that helps you take in all that amazing learning.

Think of lessons as holds on a climbing wall. If too many are missing, it makes climbing to the top really difficult, but if they're all there, it'll be easier to find a route. It's also where you can learn and practise all sorts of life skills – such as getting along with other people, communicating, teamwork, resilience and reflection – in a safe space. And then of course there's all the fun stuff, like science experiments, sports day, art projects, reading challenges, plays and school social events. There's something for everyone. When you see it all written down, it's easy to see why school can be so great!

So what I have to say is, try to make your skills useful at school, and try to do what is needed using them, but don't give up on yourself when there is a struggle.

Maybe like me, your personality makes long, quiet classes difficult, but it would be good on a podcast.

Maybe you forget instructions faster than other people, but out in the world, you will be appreciated for coming up with answers to problems.

Maybe outside the classroom you'll feel more confident to speak up and share your real self, in all its quiet glory.

Maybe you will be better at life than you are at school.

But you still have to get through school. You can try to make it enjoyable, and you have to try to stay out of trouble.

Imagine if you put five superheroes in a classroom, you would probably end up with chaos. Someone would break a desk, a laser would probably go through the wall, and you might end up with a portal to another dimension in the dinner hall. I mean, sooo cool but probably not good in real life! But if those five superheroes were each given tasks they can do really well, and the right tools to do the ones they find more challenging, just think what they could achieve!

So don't use up time and energy getting frustrated – work with your teachers and grown-ups to make the things you find hard easier, and then focus on the things you are good at.

Because you have a wonderfully wired brain, and although it might feel like your brilliant brain and the way it likes to flutter from one thing to another like a butterfly is a challenge at school, please remember that you are just getting started, my friend. And also remember that being different, like that butterfly, is beautiful.

It all comes down to communication and using the strategies we've been talking about. Help your teachers and grown-ups to help you by telling them what you need, what you struggle with, and what you love. Teachers are there to help and support you, and want to see you shine!

✹ A GOOD DAY AT SCHOOL

So the goal is to make every day a good day
at school.

Great. Easy.

Shall we go on to the next chapter?

Ermm . . . not quite.

Because the question '*How do we make every day
a good day at school?*' requires some real thinking
if we are going to answer it properly. First of all, we
need to understand what a good day at school
actually looks like for us. School can be so much
fun, and there are so many more good days than
bad days, believe me!

Do we just mean a day where we don't get in
trouble? Or do we mean a day where we are really
interested in our learning, enjoy ourselves and share
it with other people? Or a day when we speak up
and let people see how we really are?

Because a good day is about more than staying out of trouble. Sure, we can sit quietly at the back of the class staring into space and not get told off, but that doesn't sound great to me. It doesn't sound interesting, and it doesn't sound useful.
I hope you agree!

We can have a day where we are *super*-interested in our lessons. We are excitable, and maybe once or twice we have to speak with our teacher about how we can manage our excitement. Maybe we have to take a few breaks because we feel there is too much going on and can't concentrate.

Or perhaps we're so focused on a subject or task that we can't join in with the group discussion, and feel irritated when we are made to stop.

Does it have the balance between energy and calm, excitement and focus, that works for us? It is only by understanding our good days that we can learn from them, repeat them and make them happen every day.

Because if we study our good days, we can learn what went into them.

What did we have for breakfast? How did we play at break? Even what did we do before bed *last night*? If you can be a scientist of *yourself*, you can see that your good days don't just happen by luck; there are lots of different things that make them good and make them happen.

So we should study them and learn.

We also need to be more aware of the bad days and what has happened. Can you picture a bad day at school? Maybe it is *exactly* like one that someone else would say looked good. Maybe you were zoned out and silent at the back of the class. Or maybe a bad day is one where you get overstimulated and don't have a comfortable way to explain that to people, so you get frustrated.

Again, we can look at all of the choices we make on those days that don't go well and learn from

them. Did I eat a sugary cereal at breakfast? Was I on my iPad in the morning before school? Was breaktime indoors because of rain?

Knowing these things will help us make bad days less likely to happen. We should also consider how to stop them from snowballing. We have to learn about how days *become* bad days, and the points where we could step in and change something to make sure they don't get worse.

Maybe it's one conversation with your mum on the way in, or a quiet word with a teacher before class. Maybe it's fifty star jumps or a fidget spinner. We can't say yet; we have to study ourselves and our experiences to learn how we can save the day.

Last of all, we should learn about the things we enjoy about school, and think about why we enjoy them. Then we can take the enjoyable parts from some subjects and introduce them to others.

So you're ready to study yourself, your day, your tools. Then you'll be ready to level up your approach to school. And before you know it, nothing will stop you.

ACTIVITY 10
MY BEST DAY BLUEPRINT

What?

A timeline all about your day at school

Why?

To understand habits that lead to good days

How?

Draw a timeline of a really good day at school, starting from when you wake up in the morning. Label what helped it to feel good. Mention the subjects you enjoyed (maybe maths, English, PE, art) and write what made them enjoyable.

Were there relaxed moments with friends? A lunch you enjoyed or a class that you found really interesting and never wanted to end? Maybe it was one with lots of conversations and debates, or maybe it was about quiet study.

When?

NOW!

Like I said, you can only understand how to make a day good if you know what a good day really looks like. So the activity here is really important. The same can be said for the next activity, where we try to understand the hard parts of a bad day to see how they happened and how we got past them.

ACTIVITY 11
STORM LOG

What?

A timeline of a difficult day at school

Why?

To find actions to help you through a tough moment or difficult day in the future

When?

After a tough moment or difficult day

How?

Think about that tough moment:

- What can you remember happening just before?

- How were you feeling?

- What happened to change your feelings?

- What feeling showed up first?

- What helped calm you down? And if the answer is nothing, what could help?

- Is there anything that you wish you had done, or anything you wish you had had with you that could have helped? For example, a breathing break, a stress ball, a fidget spinner, a chance to explain that you wanted to take a minute outside.

I love these two activities. They are a bit like watching a sports match back to learn what went well and can be used again, and what could be better. It is only by seeing the opportunities that we missed that we can be ready to take them next time. Or by realizing what worked, so we can practise it and do it again.

And when it comes to school, this practice is super-important because it isn't easy. School is a very stimulating place, and when it comes to our ADHD, stimulation can go one of two ways. It either makes us feel pumped up or overwhelmed. So we need to understand the stimulation we get from school and learn to manage it.

✹ STIMULATION

School is a mixture of *lots* of sights, smells and sounds. There are *hundreds* of people going in different directions and doing different things. This is what is known as a *stimulating* environment.

Picture your calm corner. This is an example of a good, stimulating environment. The sounds are ones you can control, and there are no distractions or uncomfortable sensations. There is a small amount of pleasant stimulation that you choose.

Now picture a big, busy train station. There is the smell of restaurants and screech of engines, and the hustle and bustle as people push past in different directions. This is an example of an *over-stimulating* environment.

Now, we don't want *all* our life to be like our calm corner – sometimes we want it to be more like a train station, because these overstimulating spaces can also be exciting ones. We shouldn't feel worried about them.

Ideally, life should be like a train station when we need to get excited, and more like a calm corner when we need to focus or relax.

And because school is somewhere in between the calm corner and the train station, we need to think about the stimulating things we can remove when we need to feel calm, and the energy we can find when we want to get excited.

ACTIVITY 12
STIMULUS MAP

This is a bit like our Space Detective activity. It's a chance to think about all of the things in your school that you really notice.

What are the sounds that draw your attention?

Maybe it's playground noise, squeaky pens, chairs on the floor.

What are the sights?

People outside the windows? Fidgeting classmates?

What are the smells?

Lunch being cooked or maybe old school toilets (*ewww . . .*)

Think about any sense, and anything that pulls your attention in a different direction.

Lots of these things are outside of our control. If there is a PE lesson going on in the playground, we can't ask everyone to be silent for us, and we can't control whether or not the toilets are stinky. What we can do is understand how they make us feel, what we can do to feel better and how to communicate that we need some time to do whatever that is.

Trust me, it's better than shouting 'BE QUIET!' into the playground or putting a clothes peg on your nose!

So we've taken the first steps. We've noticed the different things in school and how they make us feel, and now we need to take some more time to control those feelings. Often, that will mean learning to use some new tools.

Let's look at what those tools could be, and because we spoke about how our different senses get activated at school, let's separate out the tools by sense.

✴ SOUNDS

Noise-cancelling Headphones

These are not for playing tunes but for blocking out the noises that can be overwhelming. You don't need to use them all the time, but they are a great tool to have in your bag for when you really need them.

Earplugs

These do the same, but try and use them for shorter amounts of time. This is because they can actually make us *more* sensitive if we use them all the time.

Quiet Corner

There may be a space in your classroom or inside the school that is nice and quiet. Get to know where this is, as it could be a great place to calm down. If the quiet area is outside of your classroom, and you are in a lesson, please ask your teacher first before you go!

✳ SIGHTS

Along with sound, sight can get overwhelmed in busy environments, so it's great to think about ways to feel less overwhelmed by it.

This is super important at school, as they are often very bright, buzzy spaces. Don't worry, though, because there are options.

Tinted Glasses

The first is tinted glasses. These are my FAVOURITE. If you don't believe me, check this out – once I started wearing these, I got so into them that I started my own company to make them! True story.

Tinted glasses are like sunglasses that are designed to create a calming effect. Instead of just blocking light, they change it to make it less harsh, flickery or bright. If you've ever been in a room with lots of bright artificial lights, you will know how distracting, almost *painful*, it can feel on our eyes. This is obviously not good, but when we need to concentrate on our classwork for hours at a time, it can be a real problem.

Tinted glasses smooth out the light in a way that makes it less distracting, reduces strain on our eyes and therefore means fewer headaches. They also help us to read more comfortably. This is definitely true for me. Without glasses, in bright light, the letters on a page can seem to swim around or jump, the text can go blurry, and the white background can seem too bright.

When I wear the right kind of glasses, this stops. The words stop moving, the page isn't so bright and my eyes don't hurt any more. Phew!

Overlays

These are pretty cool pieces of kit. They are simple coloured sheets of plastic that you can put over any page you are working from to make reading easier. They don't change the light; they just make a page easier to read and take in, so they are really a reading tool. I've tried these, and they really make reading much more comfortable. Find out which colour works best for you.

✺ TOUCH

Fidget spinners and other noisy tools are usually not allowed in schools, because they are distracting to other pupils – and to you! So those are best left at home. Luckily, there are lots of silent tools that are allowed with a teacher's permission. These include plain, unscented putty, tangles and chewable jewellery. You can also hold a stone with a nice texture, or use strips of felt or Velcro. Try to think about the sort of textures and materials that you like to feel against your hand. They could be added to your desk or pencil case as a tool.

The last way we can use touch to make us feel calm isn't something that we hold, but what is around us. It could be things like a lap pad at school (or a weighted blanket at home), which are heavy items that push down on your body. If you've ever got into bed and felt relaxed by how the duvet presses down on you, then you'll understand. Sometimes it feels good to have some weight on us.

These are all really useful tools that we should be happy to use. Proud, even, because we have understood ourselves and what we want. I know that isn't always easy. At first, when I started to use tools like tinted glasses to help my focus and attention, I felt a little bit embarrassed. Why did I need something that no one else did? Why did I have to be different?

But, in time, I realized that *I* don't have to be different. *Everyone does.* Some people need glasses to help them see the board, others don't. Some people get cold easily and wear their jumper, even in the summer term. Others get hot and prefer to wear shorts instead of trousers, even in February!

The point is, we all use different tools to help us feel comfortable, capable and ready, and that is great. Our differences are what make the world an interesting place, and school is a place where lots of different people meet.

We all have strengths and weaknesses, and we need the tools that maximize our strengths and protect us from the challenges our weaknesses present.

So don't worry about using the tools that help you. I know I don't. I've even started making my own!

✴ SCHOOL RESETS

The tools we use to succeed at school aren't just objects and *things*, though. They can be ideas and tricks too – resets that we turn to when we get overstimulated or under-stimulated. I have definitely learned in my life that it doesn't take much thought or effort to feel *uncomfortable* – it can happen without me noticing. But to get back on track, to feel good again – that can take a lot of work.

I can be triggered by anything, and I can lose focus without noticing it, so I need to make it easier to calm down and get focused again.

✳ **BREATHING**

Our breath is not just the source of our life and our energy; it is a direct route to our mind. I'm serious – it's like a control button or a dial that we can move and shift to change how our mind is feeling.

If we can manage our breathing, we can manage our mind.

So it's good to learn a simple breathing pattern that helps us do this. Here is my favourite. It's called box breathing.

TOP TIP

Try box breathing.

- Sit comfortably, with your eyes open or closed.

- Take an in-breath for four seconds: 1–2–3–4

- Hold it for two seconds: 1–2

- Then breathe out for six seconds: 1–2–3–4–5–6

This means you spend more time holding your breath and breathing out than breathing in, which makes us feel relaxed.

You see, panicking makes us breathe too fast – and breathing too fast makes us panic.

So we have to learn to breathe more slowly when we are feeling anxious, and turn down the dial on our stress.

✸ DYNAMIC MOVEMENT

This may sound confusing, but did you know that we can calm ourselves down by *moving fast*? Breathing slowly and moving fast, I know – weird. But really, I just mean that using up some energy can be a great way to reset and feel calmer.

So remember, at school, breaktime is a great time to get moving. The more you move around and give your energy a boost, the calmer you will feel in your next class.

But you can use movement as a reset during class too (as long as you can agree with your teacher on how to do this, which we will discuss later). For example, thirty to sixty seconds of FAST movement, like star jumps, press-ups or running on the spot, can be an amazing reset. Because I go to the gym a lot, I choose press-ups!

Now, as I said, it's important to agree with your teacher on how this will work. You can't just do star jumps in the middle of a lesson. Sorry! But if you can get a pass to go to the hall outside or have a corner of the classroom where you can go without distracting others, then movement can be a powerful reset tool.

✳ SENSORY RESETS

Those tools we spoke about, like putty, tangles or textured strips, can be used to calm our minds and focus.

If you feel yourself getting overwhelmed, close your eyes and *really zone in on that one thing*. Let your mind focus only on using that tangle, stroking that Velcro or squeezing that putty.

Maybe you set a target of a hundred strokes or fifty squeezes and then get back to your task.

✳ GROUNDING

This is another version of Pause and Notice, which we talked about earlier, but shorter, so we can do it when we don't have much time. Take a moment and close your eyes. Notice what your heartbeat feels like, whether you feel warm or cool, and what you can feel in terms of touch. Are your feet against the ground? Is there a pencil in your hand? Can you feel your school jacket against your shoulders? The main thing is switching from what you are *thinking* about in your mind to what you can *feel* with your head, hands, body or feet.

✳ COMMUNICATING

Once we have our tools, we need to feel prepared to use them, and often this means communicating with our teachers and friends about what we need.

ACTIVITY 13

CREATE A 'WHAT HELPS ME' PAGE

What?

A one-page sheet that you can share with your teachers about what helps you

Why?

Because any new teacher you work with will want to understand how to help you

How?

- Write down your **strengths**. This can include things you do well in class, such as working in pairs, quiet reading or discussions.

- Then write down your **triggers**, for example, outside noises, long periods of silence or sitting.

- Then write down your favourite **resets** from the last few pages. These could be tools like a squeezing putty, breathing exercises or dynamic movement.

- And three **requests**. For example,

   1. *When I get overwhelmed, could I take a minute to do my breathing?*

   If that doesn't work,

   2. *I might use my Velcro strip when I'm feeling fizzy.*

   And if that doesn't work,

   3. *I will put my hand up and ask if I can go outside for a break to do some dynamic movement.*

You may prefer different ways to communicate with your teacher when you have a request. That's fine, and some people like to use signals so they don't have to say these things in front of class. You can think of your own, but they could be putting your hand on your heart, tapping your wrist or raising your finger to your neck or arm to take your pulse. If you note this down, your teachers will always know what you mean.

Now, these may not always work. If they
don't, and we have a difficult moment, we
need to find a way to get back on track.

Maybe your teacher has to ask you to leave
the classroom for a break, because you didn't
catch yourself in time. That can happen, and
that's OK. It definitely happened to me, and
the important thing is that you know what you
need to do when you go outside and when
you come back in.

When you go outside, don't think of it as a
punishment. It's a reset. Do whichever of your
resets helps you the most. Then, when you
come back, always *ask your teacher* what they
would like you to do.

And repeat it back to them.

This will give you a clear explanation of what
you need to get done, and make it easier to
remember after a stressful moment.

✳ EXPLAINING

You should never feel *blamed* for getting over-stimulated or losing focus. It's part of how your brain works, and the more easily you can talk about it, the more easily everyone can understand it and learn from it.

We need blame-free ways of talking things through, and we need them to be quick and easy. Like this:

For thirty seconds (at most), you and your teacher can discuss what happened.

'I got overwhelmed during group reading.'

Then, without blaming anyone, we can describe what happened with one feeling and one fact:

'I felt fidgety (**feeling**), so I got out of my chair and walked over to the other table (**fact**).'

This doesn't need to take more than a minute.

Finally, we can make a plan for next time.

'If I feel fidgety, I'll make a signal so you know.'

Your teacher can say:

'When I see you signal, I'll give you permission to use your putty or go for a reset.'

And you can do your reset and come back, and your teacher will let you know what is needed from you. All schools have different rules about resets and leaving the classroom at certain times of the day, so it is important to agree on strategies with your teacher beforehand so that you can have different techniques to help you if going out of class is not possible.

This is *much* better than having a
stressful situation where you get
blamed or told off, and other kids
get distracted. You are doing your
best, and so is your teacher – so it's
really good to make sure doing our
best gets results.

I *wish* I had known these things at school. Man, I
wish I had known *anything* about ADHD when I was
a kid! I went through my school years feeling like I
was a *problem* because I didn't have a *solution*.
I didn't actually know I had ADHD until I became
an adult.

I was like that hero in a movie who doesn't know
they have a power and keeps breaking things,
trying to cover it up and ending up in trouble. I had
a super-strength, but I just thought I was clumsy.

You don't have to live like that. You can understand
your power and make life easier. You can make it
great. Because school is the place where you will
spend most of your time over the next few years, it's
best that you learn ways and speak with your
teachers and teaching assistants to make it a
place where you can enjoy learning and feel safe.

It is really important that you and your caregivers communicate and meet with your teachers, and teaching assistants, to talk about how they can support you. If you are diagnosed with ADHD, make sure your caregiver tells your school.

You might be like me and find that you do better outside of school. The world outside of the classroom might be a better fit for your skills, and that's cool. Or you might absolutely love classroom learning but find the social side quite tricky and overwhelming. That's cool, too – we're about to get on to friendships!

The main takeaway of this chapter is that if you understand the bits you find hard, and the ways you can make it easier, you will give yourself a lot more time to do the things that you *love* – to use your power for good.

CHAPTER 6
FRIENDS AND RELATIONSHIPS

My friends are a big part of my life. I love them.
I actually just love people in general – having a
laugh with them, playing sports and games,
creating cool things together.

But I also get seriously drained. My energy can get
super-high, but that means it can also get super-low.
A funny thing about my ADHD is that I can get
so excited around other people that I burn up
all my energy, to the point where I need a rest,
or a timeout.

This can be confusing for other people. They don't
understand that I can be so sociable that it leaves
me needing time alone.

Because in most people's minds, you are either
sociable or shy. You are energetic or lazy. You are
an out-and-about person or a homebody. But
really, we can all be both, and the more energetic
we are, the more we might need to recharge.

I like to think of it in terms of two different dogs at the park.

Most people are like those sorts of dogs you see out there who have a walk around, do a bit of sniffing, maybe run after a ball for a bit. Then go home and rest, eat a bit of dog food, have a cuddle and then feel ready to go for another walk a bit later.

That's dog **one**. Dog **A**. **TYPICO-DOGGO**.

I'm more like the other type. Dog **B**. **ADH-DOG.**

Who goes to the park and goes . . .

'RUNRUNRUNRUNRUNRUN . . . '

'FUNFUNFUNFUNFUNFUN . . .'

It sprints into the park and starts sniffing one dog, gets them excited and makes them want to play.

Then runs off to another and gets them started.

Then joins a game of football.

Runs after some joggers.

Plays with about ten different dogs at once
because they are all with a dog walker.

And then goes home annnnddd . . .

Sleeps.

For four hours. Or a whole day.

Like that dog, I can use up so
much energy connecting with
others that I need time on my own.
It can be hard for other people to
understand. They think that because I
can be a high-energy person, I will *always* be high
energy, and get confused when I go for a rest.

Because they think this means I'm not interested in
them, when really I just have to take time to
recharge my battery.

So it's been really important for me to understand
my energy levels, *learn* to keep them balanced
and **explain** when I need to take some time away.
Because I don't want to hurt people's feelings
when I go from Mr Social to Mr Distant.

And I can completely understand why that
change in my energy level can be confusing
for other people.

Imagine being Dog **A** (steady-energy dog) and meeting Dog **B** (up-and-down-energy dog) at the park. You'd *love* energy doggo. You'd think it was the best, super-fun new mate that you could play with every time you meet at the park.

But the next day, Dog **B** might be tired. It might have burned out all its energy on that first day, and now just wants to be on its own. You wouldn't blame Dog **A** for worrying that they had done something wrong – for worrying that they had offended Dog **B** or hurt its feelings.

Unless Dog **B** was able to explain.

'Sorry, bro – I just got burned out stealing all those footballs from the humans yesterday. I really need a chilled one today.'

To which Dog **A** might just say, 'That's cool. Let's just have a chilled one.'

By which I mean to say that we can learn to read our energy levels and explain to other people when they change.

We can explain that when our energy is high, we can have a good, high-energy time, and when it's low, we have a more chilled, relaxed one. It's important that our friends understand that we have not changed; our energy level has.

✸ WHY YOU CAN BE AN AMAZING FRIEND

It's because us ADHDers make great friends.

Lots of the characteristics of ADHDers are the traits of trusting, funny, loving mates. Now, you wouldn't be able to tell this from the silly name 'ADHD', which only mentions our attention (deficit) and hyperactivity (disorder? I actually feel very ordered, thanks). Whichever scientist got the chance to name it only seemed to care about how we concentrate and whether we sit still, but there is way more to us than just attention and hyperactivity.

And many of those things are *exactly* the sort of things we look for in our mates.

We also have:

- Heightened emotions
- Unique senses of humour (the best, in my opinion!)
- The ability to sense other people's feelings, called empathy and intuition
- Super creativity
- Incredible imaginations

Now look, I'm not saying
those things should **all** be
added to the term ADHD.
I understand that:
Attention Deficit
Hyperactivity Emotion
Humour Creativity
Imaginativity Disorder is
a bit too long!

ADHEHCID. Doesn't
exactly roll off the
tongue, does it?!

But it *would be* more true. Our brains *do* process
attention and energy differently, but they are also
often sensitive, funny, creative and imaginative.
And those things, if you ask me, are just as
important to who I am as the things that make me
get bored sitting behind a desk. They are the things
that make me a good friend.

Because ADHD minds are *different*, and often what
we look for in friends is the ability to think and see
the world differently. Sure, you probably share some
hobbies and habits with your friends, but we need
to have some different perspectives to make things
really interesting.

Like, imagine if you met a robot (([in your best robot

voice] *Hell-o. Nice. To. Meet. You!*) and it was programmed to think and say *exactly* the same thing as you every time you thought or spoke. You might hang out for an hour, notice a few of the same things at the park ('Hey look, a tree,' . . . 'Hey look, a tree,') or agree that you both wanted the same things for Christmas, but pretty soon you'd start to get a little bit bored.

You wouldn't find them very interesting, because they couldn't *surprise* you. We can only be surprised when someone thinks differently, so we want our friends to sometimes say things that are new to us or make us laugh with ideas we haven't thought of.

And our friends might want that from us, too. They like that we think differently, but there are actually so many other things about our ADHD that tend to make us good friends. So let's look at them, because, like all powerful things, there's a lot to appreciate and a lot to learn when it comes to super-powered friendship.

✳ HEIGHTENED EMOTIONS

We ADHDers often feel our feelings strongly. When we are happy, we can touch the sky with an infectious energy that makes everyone want to party

with us. But when we are sad or angry,
we can sometimes get darker and
spikier than other people.

Personally, I love being friends with
someone who can feel supersonic levels of
excitement and joy! Sometimes I feel it like a magnet
or an energy field – I can sense when someone is
having a good time on the other side of a room, and
my Sammy-Senses pick up on it and bring me towards
them. We have the power to light up a room, and the
power to sense someone else who is doing the same
thing when they are having fun.

Because having fun is a powerful thing. Like I said,
we are drawn to it – in the same way we are drawn
to people who are really *passionate about* certain
things.

✳ PASSION AND FOCUS

I bet you have been drawn to someone who is *hyperfocused* on something that they are passionate
about. They could be staring at ants or laying out
their football stickers, they might be thinking deeply
about their outfit or studying dinosaurs in a big picture
book. Whatever it is, when we see someone who is

super-passionate about something, we want to connect with them, understand why they are so interested in what they are looking at and learn from them.

Our ADHD means we can get super-invested in the things we care about, and friends are drawn to that. People want to share the interests we have, and that means we can be very interesting and *interested* friends.

✳ MEMORABLE MOMENTS

Our heightened emotions also allow us to create really memorable moments. If you think back to some of your best memories, they probably involved some really intense emotions. Big laughs, big joy or maybe even deep sadness when they came to an end. Because strong emotions = strong bonds = strong memories.

But of course, this means we have to be aware of strong emotions, to learn about them and manage them. It's sort of like our emotions are super-fast cars. They can speed away from other people and have bad crashes. A super-fast car is great if you know how to drive it, but you may need more time and more lessons to learn.

So we should learn about our emotions, how to manage them and how to talk to other people about them so they don't get confused when they change quickly.

We benefit, and so do our friends, if we think about how to manage our emotions and communicate about them. Then we can keep enjoying the good bits of having powerful, fast, super-car emotions and know how to hit the brakes before there is a crash.

A great way to build this skill is through **noticing**.

ACTIVITY 14

NOTICING

What?

Thinking about when you spend time with your friends

Why?

To help us notice how we are feeling with our friends, and whether we are giving them space to enjoy themselves too

How?

When you are talking with your friends, try and notice your:

- Body: *Am I leaning forward, jittery, rushing?*

- Mind: *Am I waiting to talk or listening to understand?*

- Emotion: *Am I anxious to be heard, or curious about them?*

This is great, because it is something you can do at any time to see how you are feeling and understand how you are behaving. As we said before, it's like a speedometer that tells you how fast you are travelling.

And it's great because the more we practise noticing how we feel and understanding our emotions, the better we get at it. It is by practising it when we are feeling good, excited or joyful that we become able to do it when we are feeling frustrated, withdrawn or angry.

Those can be the hardest times to check in with our emotions, but they are also the times we need it most. When we start to withdraw, feel angry or frustrated, that's when we need to stop, think and explain.

Remember the **RULER**? Yeaaahhh, you do! Have you thought of that secret hiding place yet?

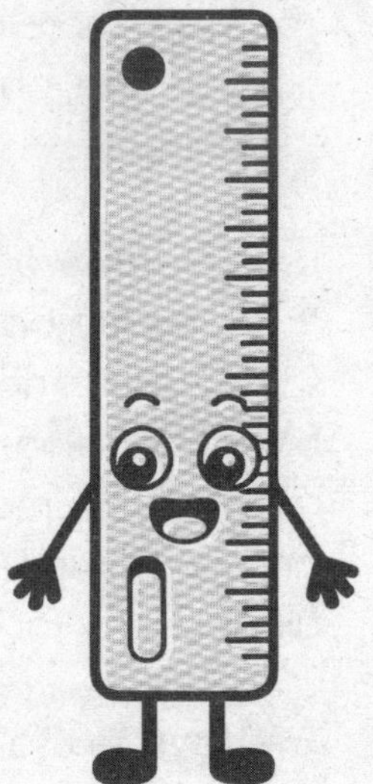

You have:

Recognized emotions building

Understood causes and effects

Labelled your emotions

Expressed them well

Regulated them

RULER.

This is exactly the sort of thing we can turn to when our emotions start to change.

Imagine you were excited about having a turn at something. Let's say you are at a funfair and going to play that game where you shoot basketballs to win a prize. You are buzzing and actually do really well to wait until your turn.

Then they skip over you to someone else. The person running it misses you out entirely.

This would be a **very** frustrating experience. I get you, trust me. It's exactly the sort of time when positive, high emotions could quickly become intense, low ones.

You were more excited than anyone else about having a go, and you are more disappointed about the unfairness.

Usually, you would get annoyed. You might start throwing the balls anyway or storm off. Maybe you shout, 'That's not fair!' This is understandable, because it's not fair. But unfortunately, it doesn't make us any more likely to get our go, win a prize and go home king or queen of the funfair with a giant bunny (or dinosaur, if that's more your thing!).

We have to use the RULER to get what we want.

Recognize the excitement building as it gets close
to our turn by noticing the feelings in our body.
Jitters in the tummy, feet are tapping, eyes are
moving and looking about from the basketballs to
the toys to the person who chooses who goes next.

Understand why this is happening. You really want
the toy. This is an exciting game. You have been
waiting a long time to have a go.

Then you get passed over for someone
else. Unfairly.

We've got to go back to **recognize**.
You might feel disappointed this time.

Understand it happened because we
got excited and then let down.

Label it as disappointment.

Express it to an adult or maybe to our friends. 'I was
meant to have the next go. I'm really
disappointed.'

Regulate: 'OK, well maybe it will be me next time.'

And, in fact, it will be *more likely* to be you next
time, because the adult you spoke to can point
you out to the person running the stall, or the friends
you explained it to might give you their turn.

But in the other situation, when you didn't recognize your feelings, you would be unlikely to get a go and even more unlikely to win a prize. You would either have stormed off or demanded your go, and then made your shots, still feeling angry or with tears in your eyes.

And no one wins the bunny when they take angry, teary shots. Believe me, I am saying this from experience!

We have to be cool (just like a cucumber), calm and collected. And that's how we win that GIANT prize.

✴ IMAGINATION, CREATIVITY AND IMPULSES

Another reason we ADHDers make super friends is that we can be mega-creative and imaginative. Ideas sort of jump into our heads out of nowhere, and other people find this really interesting.

I know for me, there is nothing more fun than coming up with ideas. Businesses, TV shows, videos online – you can find me any hour of the day coming up with suggestions for fun or interesting new ways of doing things.

I have to tell you, I'm not so great at following up on the ideas on my own. I have to find other people who are good at keeping up and finishing these ideas. I'm a great *starter*, so I appreciate people who are good *finishers*, and the good finishers are always interested in someone who can get an idea going. See, this is why I LOVE being in a team sometimes. Everyone plays a part to make that idea happen – sometimes we just need those extra-helpful hands!

Imagination and creativity are similar things that both tend to come more easily to people with ADHD. This is AWESOME: people love to be surprised by a new idea no one has ever thought of, to hear a joke that goes in a different direction or to think about something they may never have considered.

You don't need me to tell you that imaginative, creative people are fun.

But we do need to think about the flipside of imagination and creativity. This is called *impulsivity*. Now, this is a rather tricky-sounding word. Basically,

anything that we do, out of nowhere and without control, is an *impulse*.

It is a behaviour or action that just sort of happens. Now, the cool thing is that creativity and real imagination are impulsive; they just sort of happen. Many people have to struggle and think to come up with new ideas, but some – like impulsive people (like us) – find that new ideas sort of pop into their heads out of nowhere.

Impulsive people also find it hard to control what they say or do. When you get used to ideas magically popping into your head from nowhere, it can be hard to stop words popping out of your mouth, too.

Sometimes, I interrupt people.

To be fair, sometimes I interrupt *myself* – LOL!

In a way, creative ideas can sometimes just feel like a good interruption. I'm thinking about what I'm going to have for dinner and then . . . *BAM!*

'WHAT ABOUT A VIDEO GAME THAT CREATES A MOVIE WHILE YOU PLAY IT?'

Nice one, Sammy T!

Or I'm just walking to the shops and *BOOM!*

Albus and Cedric: 'Our dad is a pretty cool dude
– mega-generous with the cat treats – but we think
he should sleep more . . . like we do!'

OK, to be honest, the first one is a good idea (an
interruption). The second one is more just like . . .
funny? But I don't mind it. Basically, what I am
saying is that interruptions in an ADHD mind can
spark great ideas, funny jokes or interesting points
of view on something.

But interruptions in a conversation can sometimes
make *other* people feel hurt.

You see, to us, an interruption is a sign that
something interesting is happening, but for another
person, it might feel like a sign that you don't find
them interesting. They might feel hurt that you are
not listening and are more interested in *speaking*.

The funny thing is, for me, an interruption is like a
sneeze (errr . . . bless you!). I can sort of feel it build
up. This is good, because it means I can sense it
and then **communicate** to another person that I
need to say something. Just like you might reach for
a tissue before you sneeze, you can signal to
another person when you want to interrupt.

The first thing is to let people know what it means when you interrupt.

You could say: *'Sometimes I jump in because I get excited – it's never to talk over you.'*

That's a great start, because it means you can let someone know *when* you are excited to get involved in the conversation. You can do this with a gentle, private signal. Maybe you tap the table or raise your finger, if it is a private conversation.

Or you can raise your hand if it is a teacher. It's best to agree on this before conversations or classes, then the other person knows you are not trying to *stop them* speaking – only to *join them* – they are more likely to say something like 'One second, then it's your go,' or 'I'm almost done, then you can jump in.'

And you can focus on breathing carefully and waiting your turn.

At the end of the chat, it's great to let someone know that you found it an exciting and interesting conversation.

You see, talking to someone who is excited and enthusiastic (which means passionate about something) is GREAT. Speaking to someone who speaks over us and won't let us finish our point is RUBBISH. So we have to find the good bits of enthusiasm and manage the challenges of over-enthusiasm when it spills into careless chat.

If that does happen, and we do hurt someone's feelings by interrupting, it's OK. We can repair this by apologizing and focusing. By saying something like, 'Sorry, I got over-excited – go ahead,' or 'Wow – this is so interesting. I sometimes jump in when I'm really focused on something.'

I've had to learn to do this. I had to learn to take a breath (1-2-3-4 . . . *ahhh!*) when I'm listening, and take my time when I'm talking about something that gives me lots of energy. This is another example of when the skill of noticing is super-important. If I can notice that I am getting energized by something, that I am rushing ahead talking about it, then I know to take a look and see that other people need a turn to talk.

Because it's great that I have the power to speak passionately about things I'm interested in, but I don't want my superpower to make other people feel left out. So I have to make space for them. The last thing I want to do is hurt someone's feelings by making them feel ignored.

✴ FAST FRIENDSHIP

The thing about having the power of super-emotion, though – high and low – is that friendships can be *powerfully* fun, and sometimes *powerfully* disappointing.

Like lots of other ADHDers, I have the ability to make friends *super*-fast – and *super*-strong. This is a sort of power, like hyper-speed for social connection. I can meet someone and chat for an hour and feel like we've been friends forever. I love that. It feels special, and it can make other people I connect with feel special, too.

The danger is that I can go from connecting really fast to feeling a bit more distant. It's not that I stop liking people as much, or that I want to push them away; it's just that *getting to know someone* can be exciting in itself. This means that once we know each other, I might be a bit less excited.

Unfortunately, this means that a strong skill for making connections can feel like a super-let-down for

someone else when I seem like I've gone off them.

But it doesn't have to be a big problem. I've learned to tell people when my energy is a bit lower, or I feel like I need to recharge my battery. I don't feel afraid to tell people that it might *seem* like I'm less enthusiastic, when really I just need some time by myself.

Usually, they understand, but if they don't, then I have to realize that's OK too. You see, if I connect fast with someone and then need space to recharge, and they find that too up-and-down, too fast-and-slow, or too hot-and-cold, I have to respect that. It might just mean we are not a good friendship match. If my energy levels make them feel rejected and there isn't a way for me to explain myself, then I realize I have to find other people who better match my energy.

Of course, this is just one side of friendships for ADHDers. Perhaps you're quiet and feel a bit worried about making friends. You may come across as shy and feel unsure about sharing your interests and ideas, and find it easier to have a smaller friendship group – which is totally cool, too! Or you may be masking and copying others to fit in, rather than letting your fizzy flag fly.

ADHD can show up in so many different ways, which is what makes you so unique and special – and such a great friend. My best friends are some of the most important people in my life, and they understand me and my ADHD. They love me for who I am. They are legends . . . and don't forget to tell your mates that, if they are too! It will make them feel good.

☀ MASKING

So now we know that ADHD brains work differently to neurotypical brains. And every person with ADHD is a unique and awesome person, and ADHD might show up in different ways for each individual person. Sometimes we can try and pretend, blend in and be like everyone else. This is called masking. It's kind of like acting, where you play a character and try to copy other people. Sometimes people who mask work hard to keep all of their uniqueness hidden under a cloak of normality (a bit like a cloak of invisibility!). But instead of making you disappear, this one makes you appear super 'normal' and like everyone else.

Many superheroes – Spider-Man, Ms. Marvel, Batgirl and loads of others – lead a sort of double life. One where they are 'normal' (whatever that means!) and another where they are super and use their differences to do great things.

Now, I don't believe there is such a thing as normal, but I definitely spent a lot of time wishing I was the same as everyone else when I was a kid... If you've done this before, then please remember, you are not alone. Holding all your emotions in all day is exhausting. Trust me, you will feel a lot better if you open up to an adult about how you are feeling, and they will support you.

✳ REJECTION SENSITIVITY

Here's a hard truth: not everyone will want to be friends with you. There, I've said it. But the thing to remember is that this is *true for everyone*. I already feel better – about when I get rejected, and when I come across as rejecting other people. Though I really understand people's sense of sadness that they sometimes feel about rejection. Like lots of other ADHDers, I have a thing called 'rejection sensitivity' – which means we feel extra hurt when we think other people don't feel as positively or strongly about us as we feel about them.

There are parts of having ADHD
that I love and are what make
me a great friend, brother
and son. But rejection
sensitivity is a bit of my
ADHD that I find really hard
sometimes. You might find
another part of your ADHD
tough, and it's OK to feel
that way. However, your
friend Sam here wants to say
don't be afraid to talk about it
with a trusted grown-up or friend.

I heard someone say once that it's like we ADHDers
live in HD (like the best TV screen you have EVER
seen, where you can see every tiny thing on the
screen clearly). We can sense every vibration, see
every detail and hear every sound in greater detail
and at greater volume.

But that means we can be super-sensitive to things
being even a little bit wrong. For example, if
someone does what we just spoke about doing
ourselves – if they connect with us really fast to make
a friendship, and then slow down a bit – I feel that
super-strongly. It's an example of rejection sensitivity.

I feel like they've rejected me. Told me I'm not
good enough. Sometimes, it feels like I'll never
be good enough.

I've taken something small, something that may not even be true, and built it up into a much bigger, much sadder story about me. Luckily, as always, there are ways we can make this hard part of our difference just a little bit easier. The first thing is simply knowing it is a part of our ADHD.

Being able to say 'My ADHD makes me feel things strongly. That's what I'm struggling with now, as I feel rejected.'

You see, I didn't know I had ADHD until I was nearly thirty, and it was learning to explain why some things felt so strong that helped me the most. So instead of not being in control of my emotions, it went something like this:

1. I feel hurt.

2. Why do I feel so hurt?

3. Why does no one else
   seem to feel so hurt?

4. Why am I so odd and different?

5. I feel hurt that I'm odd and different
   (and back to step one . . .)

Now I could go:

1. I feel hurt.

2. Why do I feel hurt?

*Because I'm disappointed that someone isn't
as excited about our friendship as I am.*

3. Why do I feel sooo hurt?

Because I have a particularly sensitive brain.

I could stop the spiral because I could explain the
feelings and why they were so strong. I could also
remind myself that I wasn't a special case, a one-off,
or the *only person in the world
who felt that way.*

I had a chance to see that
there are loads of people out
there like me, and that we
aren't victims – we are just
able to sense the world in an
extra-powerful way. Then I
had to start using new
approaches to help
myself feel less hurt,
for less time.

The first step is to ask if I have *actually* been rejected. You see, we ADHDers are sensitive, but that doesn't mean we are always *right*. Sometimes there are false alarms, and it helps to check whether we are just imagining that our friends have rejected us.

I try and think about what the other person has done that has made me feel rejected, and then ask if I have ever behaved that way. Then I try to think about whether I could behave that way without *meaning* to make someone feel rejected. And if I'm struggling, then I open up and talk to someone about how I'm feeling, and I urge you to do the same. If you are having a tough time with feeling rejected, then speak to a trusted grown-up, and they will be able to support you through it.

Usually, I realize that people aren't *trying* to reject me or hurt my feelings. I'm just very sensitive, and I see that as a good thing. Who wouldn't want an ultra-HD TV screen, right?! It's good to be sensitive to kindness and hurt feelings, and it's a super-strength if we put it to good use.

I try to use that power to notice when people might feel left out, or to help people who have been rejected feel involved. The worst thing I can do is use my sensitivity to feel sorry for myself for things that haven't happened. That is a waste of my precious

time and energy, so I try to use it, like all good people, to help others.

✳ PAYING ATTENTION

This means paying attention. Now, I know we started this chapter by saying that the name ADHD is a bit basic – that it talks about attention and hyperactivity and ignores all the good stuff. But I have to admit . . . sometimes I struggle to pay attention to other people for a long time.

And that's cool. It's sort of the price I pay for having a mind that can jump around in different directions.

Think about it, a superhero with the power to jump up to the top of a skyscraper would probably struggle to sit still, and a mind that can leap up to the sky often doesn't stay still in one place.

It sounds like a great skill for me, at least, but it's not fair on the person that I'm leaping away from. You see, I expect people to listen to me when I'm speaking to them, so I think it's only fair that I listen to them too.

This is hard, but it's not impossible for ADHDers like me. I just have to make an effort and use some useful tricks.

Firstly, and we've sort of spoken about this already, it really helps to have something to fidget with in my hands. Sometimes I hold a chess piece or a fidget spinner, anything to allow me to wander with my hands so that my attention can stay in one place.

Secondly, I use mindful listening tricks. I try to focus my attention on someone's face, or the hand gestures, and then when they finish a point, I sum it up in my head (*'So she's saying she misses her cousin,'* or *'Pete feels left out.'*). Then I usually try to ask one question. This is something simple like 'Oh, what do you miss most about your cousin?' or 'How could we make you feel more involved, Pete?'

By thinking about our question when we are listening, we allow our mind to be creative and go in other directions, but it is directed *towards* what the other person is saying.

But if that doesn't work, and I do lose attention, I'm not afraid to say 'Sorry, I lost you during that last bit, can you repeat from . . .' and then mention the last thing I remember.

Because people don't mind that my attention is different, that I get excited, or that I can be sensitive to rejection. They just want to feel like I understand them, care about them and value them.

Because we ADHDers can be the funniest, most creative and loving friends. We bond really strongly, and we feel things really deeply.

But we do all of that differently, and our lives and our power will all be appreciated much more if we have the tools and take the time to explain that.

Nice one, mate!

CHAPTER 7
ORGANIZATION

Wait, wait, wait – don't close the book. I know that a chapter called *Organization* sounds like the most BORING thing in the world, but trust me, it's not!

The most boring thing in the world is being told for the five thousandth time that you've forgotten something. That you're disorganized. That you need to *be more like him or her or whoever*, who doesn't forget stuff and always gets it done on time.

Sure, organization may not be the most exciting subject in the universe, but disorganization really isn't either. So let's talk about being organized – so no one ever needs to talk *at us* about being disorganized!

For me, this subject is *personal* because in my life,
I have been called all of the following things:

- disorganized (obviously!)

- forgetful

- scatterbrained

- away with the fairies

- lost

- careless

- slapdash

- slipshod (nah, I'm not sure what that
  means either, to be fair . . . it's apparently
  being sloppy with things!)

- jumbled

- muddled

- chaotic

- cluttered

- shambolic (messy in how you act)

- higgledy-piggledy

- absent-minded

- unreliable.

And that was pretty much just at school. But worst
of all, I heard all those things, and I *believed* them.
I thought I was the most forgetful, unreliable,
shambolic higgeldy-pig ever born, but really
that was wrong.

I just had ADHD, and if I had known I had ADHD,
I could have learned tricks and tools to help myself
and know that it wasn't just me who had these
difficulties. I wasn't uniquely jumbled or muddled.
I was just part of a group of people who approach
time and organization differently.

Because we ADHDers have a habit of living in the
moment. Which is a good thing! Many people
recommend living in the moment as a way to live
a happy life. And yet . . . people can seem quite
frustrated when we pay a little bit less attention
to planning for the future.

Or when we are more interested in kicking a ball
now than packing a bag for tomorrow, or stroking a
cat *(MEOWW!)* now, rather than thinking about how
long we will need to get all our homework done.

I would love to live in a perfect little world, where
everyone just climbs trees and strokes cats, but I've
realized that there is a good reason to think about
the future. Someone has to think about getting food
for that cat or making sure that the sports shops

stock footballs. We can't all just live in the moment, because each moment depends a little bit on someone in the past who prepared for it when it was the past.

So we have to learn about organization, and a great thing for me when I found out I had ADHD was that I discovered all these tips and tricks to help me be more organized – all the tools and skills to make organizing easier. After years of thinking I was a bit ramshackle (another grown-up word! It means being a bit of a mess in how you act) and disorganized – forever and no matter what – I learned that I just needed a bit of help and a bit of practice.

So let's get down to business (or organization . . . or planning).

✴ PLANNERS AND CALENDARS

Do you lurrrrrrve your planner?

I do. I know it sounds a bit funny, but it genuinely changed my life. Up until I got diagnosed with ADHD, I never had one – I never planned my weeks or days or months, and basically my whole life came as one big surprise.

Every morning was like, wake up, brush teeth, then – *WHAM!* – here's a thing I was meant to do that I forgot about. Every day basically included one moment where my stomach dropped, and I thought, *'Oh no, I completely forgot about that . . . doh!'* It is not a fun way to live your life.

Then, through the clouds, on the back of a beautiful winged horse, surrounded by choirs of angels going 'Aaaaaaaah,' appeared . . . my calendar.

(Angelic choir continues to sing 'aaaaaaaah!')

And dude, it saved me. It saved me from that stomach-dropping feeling. It saved me from letting someone I cared about down. It saved me from feeling like I was all those names that I got called.

Instead, it made me feel prepared, and feeling prepared made a huge difference. Prepared means putting *everything* in there. Even things that I do *every day*. So, for example, I like to go to the gym every morning – what can I say, I like being fit and strong! I don't need to remind myself of that, but I put it in my calendar.

That might seem pointless, but I don't think it is. You see, the calendar or planner isn't just about reminding yourself; it's about seeing it. My calendar lets me see what my day looks like (busy!), think about what it will feel like (maybe quite tiring?) and then helps me make decisions about what should go in based on that (maybe keep some time free in the evening to relax, as I will be pooped and need to rest).

My calendar is like X-ray specs that allow me to see through walls, or a super-powered device that helps me understand the future.

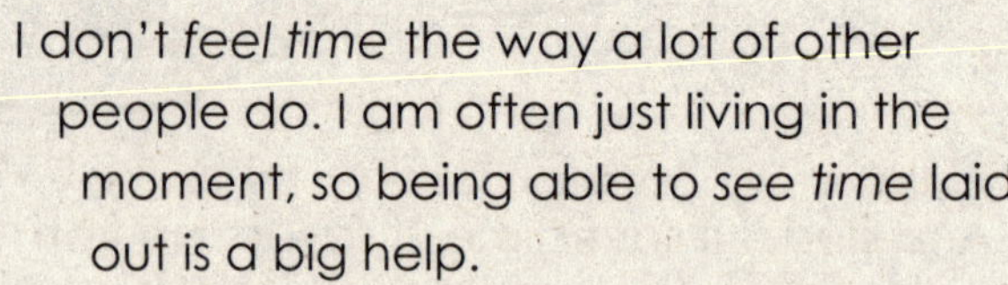

I don't *feel time* the way a lot of other people do. I am often just living in the moment, so being able to *see time* laid out is a big help.

I now know that people with ADHD often find that having a routine is really important. If they know what's going to happen next, they can be prepared for it.

You might find that
writing things down,
particularly writing
down your daily
routine, might be
a huge help.

✳ CHUNKING

And that's why I like to break up my days, my
projects and even the small things that I have to
do, into parts or chunks that I can easily manage.
There are a few different ways to think about this.

One is the big chunks: the ways we break up our
days. So, for example, if I look at my calendar, it is
broken down into hours and even half-hours. That's
great when it comes to planning a day. I don't
want to be putting down what I'm doing every five
minutes or five seconds (like breathe in . . . breathe
out), but I do like to have four or five things on my
calendar to show me the main points for that day.
That's how to chunk a day.

But I also like to chunk individual tasks in the day.
My brain, like those of a lot of ADHDers, can freeze
when I have a big task without a clear endpoint. So
I like to break things down into short, clear chunks

so I can finish them and give myself
a pat on the back. *Good job, Sam!*

If I have something that will take an
hour, I might take it five minutes at a
time. I like five minutes. It's a time period
that works for me when I have a task, but you might
be different. I use a little timer that I set for five
minutes and turn it on to get started. Instead of
saying to myself, 'I'm going to get this done,' I say, 'I'll
do this for five minutes,' and start my timer.

Usually, when I come to the end of the five minutes,
I'm feeling fine and ready to go again. Instead of
looking at a *whole big task* and thinking 'I'll never get
that done,' I think 'Can I do five minutes more?' and
each time, I usually think, 'yeah!' – up until the point
where the task *is done*.

✴ PRIORITIES (IMPORTANT THINGS TO DO)

But how do we know which task is the most
important? I sometimes find this hard to decide,
because everything can seem interesting or urgent
depending on how you look at it.

But I have to ask myself, 'What would make the biggest
difference if I got it done today/now?' I have to sort the

things on my list from urgent through to important, down to just good to get done. I usually only allow myself three things that I call urgent or important on any day, and these I put in my 'cheat sheets'.

The cheat sheets flew in on the winged horse just after the calendar (by which I mean that my doctor gave them to me!), and I love them just as much. They are simple but really helpful. Each night, I take my cheat sheet and write down the three things that I need to get done the next day. Easy-peasy.

So simple, it feels like cheating. But it's not – it's *sheeting*.

✸ REWARDS AND GAMIFYING

Then whenever I tick off the items on my cheat sheet, or anything I marked as something to get done in my calendar, I reward myself. I LOVE this! I can reward myself after a five-minute chunk well done, a task completed or after all three of my cheat-sheet priorities get done.

What matters is that I have paired a good effort with a nice reward. It can just be a 'well done', a stretch break or a snack. I could do a bit of movement, or even tick it off on my planner to give

me a sense of accomplishment. The best thing is seeing that tick on my list – it makes me feel good.

What matters is that my brain, and lots of ADHD brains, really responds to fast feedback. Instead of waiting weeks or months to be told we're doing a good job, we like to remind ourselves regularly that we are getting things done.

If life was a video game, then non-ADHDers would be happy to play one of those open-world games where you are always building and progressing towards a final goal.

But we ADHDers want short, sharp levels. We want to complete a level every five minutes. We want some feedback that says we've won.

And thinking about school work in terms of a game can be *really* useful. There are apps such as Brili Routines and OurHome out there that literally make a game from your tasks. You put your tasks into it, and then you earn badges when you complete them, and lose them when you do things you want to avoid (like eat junk food). That's pretty cool, but you don't have to use an app. You can get creative and design your very own chart on a piece of card or paper at home to stick on a wall in your bedroom or on the fridge.

You can always give yourself your own rewards for completing tasks, and even better, change the rewards depending on how well you do them. Maybe you set a timer for twenty minutes to complete your homework, or have a goal of zero spelling mistakes. Maybe you can make your test revision into a quiz!

Whatever it is, think about what you enjoy about games and try to bring that into the things you need encouragement to do. It will help keep you motivated and focused.

✳ YOUR ENVIRONMENT

This isn't a biggie, because we've already talked about how your spaces can affect your focus, but try to be aware of the sort of space you are in when you are trying to complete a task.

If you have set yourself a goal, for example, to do your homework in thirty minutes or tidy your room to gain some XP, think about whether or not you are *starting* with distractions.

Are there noises that you could do
without that might distract you?

Is your desk covered with
different, distracting things?

Are you trying to get something
done in a busy place when there are
other, more peaceful places you could go?

What we do and how we do it are important, and
where and when make a big difference to how
comfortable it all feels.

✳ REMINDERS, CHECKS AND MEMORY BUDDIES

And at the end of all this, we have set ourselves
up for success.

We have succeeded in preparation, and as a
result, we are prepared to succeed.

We are much less likely to forget or fail to complete
important tasks if we follow the steps mentioned
so far:

- Planners/calendars

- Breaking tasks into chunks

- Deciding on what is important to do first

- Giving ourselves positive feedback and creating a fun game to finish a job

- Making sure we have a good environment

But that doesn't mean we will *never forget or never struggle*.

You can use things like tick lists to help you have visual reminders of what is left to do and anything you might have forgotten. It gives you a nice sense of satisfaction when things get done, but it also helps work out *what is most important*. Your tick list shouldn't say things like 'FOCUS!' but clear and possible tasks like 'get history homework done'. This will give you that hit of satisfaction when the task is complete.

It will also remind you when a task remains *uncompleted*. Another great way of remembering things we need to get done is putting sticky notes in places that you often go, to remind you of the most important things. I have these all over my house!

You could have different colour notes for different levels of importance: red = now, yellow = soon, blue = if I have time.

These are called memory aids, or buddies, as I like to call them, and they turn the things we might forget into things we can **see**. This works for me, because as I said, I live in the moment and part of any present moment (right now) is *what I can see in front of me.*

So I make it work for me. I think living in the moment and being sensitive to the things that are happening around me as part of my superpower. It makes some things more difficult, though, like remembering what I need for the next day or getting slightly boring tasks done, but that's a fair trade. I like my brain; I like how I notice things – I just have to work with it and organize the world around it.

I may not be the most organized person, but I should never have to feel:

- forgetful

- scatterbrained

- away with the fairies

- lost

- careless

- slapdash

- slipshod

- jumbled

- muddled

- chaotic

- cluttered

- shambolic

- higgledy-piggledy

- absent-minded

- unreliable.

I just live in the moment. And every moment, in every chunk of every day, I get better.

Better at helping myself. Better at helping others. And better at helping others help me. And you can too. You've already started. Well done, you!

See, you've just read a whole chapter on organization. You can do anything. Oh, the power!

CHAPTER 8

FOOD, SLEEP AND EXERCISE

Food was never really something I thought about when I was younger. It was just sort of there. I knew I needed it, sometimes I wanted it, but I didn't spend my time thinking about it. The same for sleep. Until I got my ADHD diagnosis, I thought sleep was just something we all had to do. It wasn't something I could try and improve to have a happier, healthier life.

Food and sleep were just like *air* to me. I needed them; I'd *definitely miss them* if they were gone. But I wasn't gonna start planning my life around having high-quality fresh air (two tickets to the mountains, please!).

What I didn't know was that healthy food and sleep are mega-important for ADHDers, but we don't always have a clear idea of how hungry and tired we are.

This is because ADHD changes how we sense and *feel* our bodies. This is called 'interoception' (woahh, big old word there!) and it's basically the sixth sense, after:

- Sight

- Taste

- Hearing

- Smell

- Touch

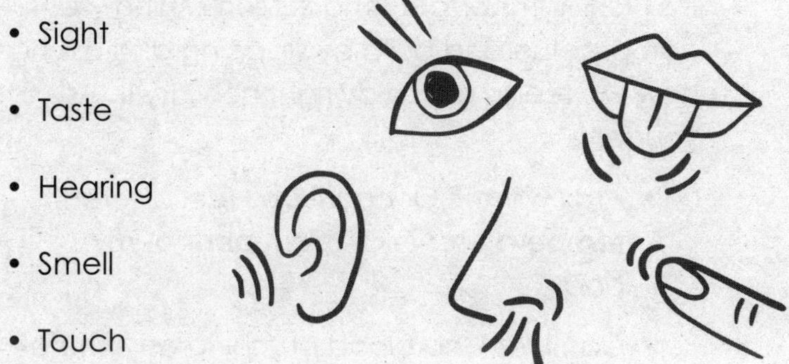

And we ADHDers can be sort of super when it comes to these senses. We can be extra sensitive (remember the ultra-HD TV we talked about?) to the smallest sounds or notice smells that others don't, which is cool. It can also get us overstimulated a lot of the time, which can really disrupt our day.

But it seems that this means we can be *less* sensitive to what we are feeling *inside*. You see, the five senses deal with the outside world and how our body connects to it, but interoception is about feeling *how we are feeling*.

TOP TIP

It's PRETTY important, and it's something we can practise and build by stopping and asking how we feel in our body right now. Try it. Ask yourself:

- *Am I warm? Or cool? Do I feel different temperatures in different parts of my body?*

- *Can I feel the blood pumping anywhere? In my hands? Or at my heartbeat?*

- *Does my stomach feel full? Or empty? Has it made a noise?*

- *Do I feel calm or jittery? Do my toes want to tap, and do my hands want to fidget?*

It's a small activity, but it builds up the sense of what's inside, which is super-important when it comes to eating and sleeping well and for using our energy to achieve our goals.

✸ EATING AND DRINKING (MUNCH, MUNCH, MUNCH . . . GULP, GULP, GULP!)

You see, when it comes to eating and drinking, we need to understand what's going on in our bodies to know what we need and when we need it. Think about when you're in a car. Whoever is driving has to stop and get petrol, because that is the fuel that makes the car run.

But the driver has to *know* when the fuel needs replacing, because the car can't move when there's no fuel in it! There has to be some way of checking how much fuel is in the car, and a way of showing when it needs to be topped up. If we don't work on 'interoception', we are like a driver without a fuel gauge. We risk rushing around and then realizing we have run out when we are *nowhere near* a petrol station.

For ADHDers, that means realizing we are hungry or thirsty before it's too late and finding out there isn't any healthy food or drink available. When I used to forget to eat or drink, I would get shaky and grumpy. I couldn't focus and would become snappy or angry much more easily. Booooo! All of the things that people misunderstand about ADHD (distraction, misbehaving) would come through,

and all the awesome things (the hyperfocus and creativity) would disappear.

That's true for anyone, but for us ADHDers it's super-important. Our focus is something we have to protect; our moods are too powerful to be forgotten, and these are things that get affected when we forget to eat. We also think less clearly and make not so good decisions when we are hungry, so I think we can agree that eating well (and eating before we get hungry) is a good idea.

But how do we do it?

Well, for me, I set reminders about food and decide on the meals and snacks I will have long before I need them. This might sound tricky, but it's as simple as knowing 'I have porridge and bananas for breakfast and I always carry an apple with me.'

That. Is. Top-notch. Eating.

And it's simple. Sometimes people make it sound complicated to eat in a healthy way, but it isn't really. Try to have some healthy food with you most of the time. Try to eat meals that involve lots of vegetables and protein (which comes from meats, fish or beans) and choose snacks that are fruits or nuts.

If you like, you can just use my simple test. This will tell you if a meal is the real deal:

TOP TIP

- Ask yourself: *Was this food made in a factory?* If the answer is no, it passed the first test.

- Then ask: *Does this meal have some protein?* If it's a yes, it passed the second. Protein is an important food group to help you grow and be STRONG.

- Finally: *Are there fruits or vegetables that still look like fruits or vegetables?* If it's a third yes, then congratulations – you've won! (Winner, winner, chicken/chickpea dinner!)

Your real meal is the real deal and you can feel real *(happy squeal!)* about your meal deal.

If you keep healthy snacks with you, you're less likely to crash. If you don't crash, your mind will be clear, and you'll easily be able to focus long

enough to do this test when it comes to your next meal – and keep going on and on in a beautiful cycle of healthy ADH-*eating*. Of course, it's pretty unlikely that you buy all the groceries in your house – I mean, you're a kid, after all! – so how do you go about getting the foods you need? Well, as usual, it's all about communicating with your grown-ups. Communication is key, as I like to say! Now that you know what sorts of foods you want and need, share that information with them.

If you hate mushrooms but discover one day that you actually quite like the delicious tiny trees of broccoli, then maybe ask for extra broccoli in the school canteen. Or if you find your tummy is rumbling and you are absolutely starving by the time lunch comes round at school, ask if you can take a banana in your school bag, and have it as a healthy snack at break time. Trust me, your brain will thank you when it comes to that pesky spelling test just after lunch break and you have fuelled yourself with all the delicious nutrients that come in bananas and broccoli. Ask if you can have a crisp, juicy apple in your lunchbox instead of a processed cereal bar, and a chunk of cheese instead of a packet of crisps.

I've gone through plenty of times where I've felt like all I wanted was sugary and salty snacks, but I feel so much better and more energized when I make these simple swaps.

But you want to know what's really cool? What we eat doesn't just change how we feel when we are awake; it also changes how we get that much-needed sleep.

✴ SLEEP . . . ZZZZZZZ!

Because, basically, our bodies have their own calendar and clock inside of them. They don't think of time in terms of hours and minutes, but in terms of day and night or waking and sleeping. It makes us feel sleepy when it thinks it's night-time. It decides it is night-time (because it doesn't have an actual clock), based on:

- When we wake up

- When we eat our meals

- The light that we see

Which, I know, sounds strange! Like, *surely our body knows it's night-time . . . when it's night-time.* Right?

Well, yes . . . and no. Our eyes can tell if it's day or night, but our bodies actually need a bit more information. Think about it – it can be dark at 4 p.m. in January, that's night-time, but we don't all want to be falling asleep at 4 p.m. So we need a bit more info.

Our bodies don't just want to know it's night, but that it's *bedtime*. That is down to it getting dark, and also these other things:

1. When we wake up, and in particular when we first see daylight. This is what tells our body clock to start the timer – it's like an on button.

That's why I try to get up and out so that I see the sun soon after I wake up. This means I will feel more ready to sleep when it comes to bedtime.

2. When we eat. I try to eat my meals at the same time each day. This tells my body that everything is on schedule.

7:00 a.m. – wake up

7:15 a.m. – see sunlight
and do some exercise

8:30 a.m. – breakfast

I keep my schedule similar
for lunch and dinner too.

1:00 p.m. – lunch

4:00 p.m. – snack

7:00 p.m. – dinner

This is so my body feels like the day is moving
forwards and it will be bedtime a few hours later
(my usual time is 10 p.m., three hours after dinner).
I hope you don't go to bed this late, though! My
body, like my brain, likes a schedule, and it can
schedule bedtime more easily if everything else is
on time.

OK, so that covers when we wake up and the
timing of our meals. But what about the third thing?

3. The light that we see.

Well, we talked about how seeing natural sunlight
in the morning sort of starts your timer for the day,
and seeing that it has become night-time gives
your body an idea that it is time to feel more
sleepy, but we also have to think about unnatural
light, such as lights in our house, on our phones or
our TV screens.

Because our body can't really tell the difference between the light from the sun and the light from a phone screen; if I look at social media at 9 p.m., I'm basically telling my body *HELLO, IT'S DAYTIME!*

Which is weird, I know. It would be nice if my body could tell the difference between my phone light and sunlight, but it just can't. So I have to be really careful about the lights I see in the evening. I try to make my house lights a little dimmer at night, more like the colours you would see at sunset, and I don't use screens in the hour before bed. You should try the same thing – it really helps me get to sleep quicker.

This might sound like a lot to think about, but for me it's worth it. I struggle if I have a bad night's sleep, and for a long time I actually struggled to sleep *at all*.

For about two years, I would get so jittery and anxious in bed that I would struggle to sleep. Then I would start to worry if I would *ever sleep again*. This only meant I had a whole new thing to be jittery and anxious about, and it would keep me up even longer. In the end, I could go for whole nights without sleeping, feel terrible the next day and then only manage to sleep the next night because I was exhausted.

So I learned ways of making myself calmer:

- Relax before bed

- Lower lights and no screens

- A good routine from the morning that meant my body knew to feel tired at bedtime.

And finally, exercise – which also helps me eat and sleep better.

✸ EXERCISE

Exercising, sleeping and healthy eating are like a triangle of good things for me. They all help me feel better, and they all help me do the other things better, too.

When I sleep well, I make good decisions about what to eat, and I wake up feeling energized and ready to exercise. When I eat well, I can exercise more and recover faster, and also sleep better at the right time.

All three things sort of swirl into one and make me a happier, healthier person. They can really feel like the difference between my ADHD being the

problem that so many people think it is, and the *amazingly awesome* thing I know it can be. I eat, sleep and move to make my life better, and that's cool because life is all about eating, sleeping and moving. Simples!

And moving is something all of us can enjoy for sure. Maybe you aren't into sports, but what about having a dance? If you don't like dancing, have you ever been so excited by something that you've just run towards it? Or maybe you've played games, like toilet tag or duck-duck-goose?

Moving can be anything we want it to be, and it might just be the most important thing for my ADHD. You see, all people are supposed to move. We are animals. We need to move around. It's just that these days we don't have as much reason to. Movement looks different for different people, but anything you can do counts!

We are expected to sit down at school. To wait at the table for dinner. To get in the car and drive to our friends' houses or see family at the weekends. We are expected to sit still much more than we are expected to move around, and that is hard for lots of people. Me in particular! So I have to make sure *I make time to move*, as everyone else seems to want me to sit down.

And too much sitting around makes me fidget. So I
go and exercise *first thing in the morning*. That way,
nothing can come up in my day and get in the
way; no one can *demand* that I sit still and forget
about exercising. I get it done, for me.

It's because I love it, but also because it's good for
my heart, good for my muscles and good for my
mind. If I have exercised, then my energy and my
focus feel more balanced for the day, I don't have
as many big spikes or drops, and I just feel a bit
more chilled out.

TOP TIP

If I could recommend one thing for you, it's trying to
exercise each morning. Tell your grown-ups that
you want to run around the block, or the park, or
do a thousand star-jumps. Or it might be that you
walk, cycle or scoot to school. Decide that you
want to get strong and start doing press-ups.
Whatever it is, if it's exercise, it's going to help, and
you should do it **every morning**.

I'm not kidding. Say it with me. I will walk or I will run,
I will skip, jump or lift, EVERY MORNING!

Because it's a great thing for your body, your ADHD mind and your life. It's real activity, outside, with other people around.

And as we know, we spend a lot of our time these days inside and on screens. That has its benefits, but it has its problems too. So we ADHDers have to make time to get away from the world of screens, and exercise is my *favourite* way.

So come on, let's get moving, guys . . . woohoo!

TECHNOLOGY, THE INTERNET AND GAMES

I'm a gamer.

Ever since I was a kid, I've always played on a console or PC. From strategy games where I carefully create whole cities and civilizations to fast-paced, first-person shooters where my heart is beating so fast that I'm on the edge of my seat!

I love it, and I've always loved it. I think I always will. I've also had to learn how to game in ways that allow me to enjoy the rest of my life and keep my mind and body healthy.

I try to avoid playing them before bed or for too long without breaks. I also have friends who feel overstimulated or get super tired if they game for too long. Every person is different.

It's similar to social media. My job is on the internet and on apps like Instagram and TikTok. They are amazing, and I would never have been able to communicate with so many people without them, but I have had to learn how to use social media in a way that feels healthy.

This might sound like video games and social media can make you *sick*, but that's not really my point. What I mean is that gaming, when done for the right amount of time (a few hours a week, maybe), can be a good thing. It is relaxing, sociable and exciting.

But they are both types of
technology that are made to
make us lose track of time. You
might have had a moment where
you looked up from YouTube or
your favourite video game and
realized hours had passed without you noticing it.
That's because they are disconnected from the real
world and are designed to keep us away from reality.

So it's good to understand how much we are using
them and whether they are getting in the way of
other things that we could be doing – things that
might make us feel more connected to our friends,
physically healthy, or happy because we are
learning new skills.

This is extra important for ADHDers like us.

You see, my brain is always looking for something
interesting. Which is great! It's like that person in a
friendship group who is always suggesting new
games, looking for new places or finding things to do.

It is always on the lookout and attracted to the
brightest, flashiest things.

Video games and social media are *designed* to be
those sorts of bright, flashy things, and they are

designed to keep giving us little boosts that make us want to keep using them. If I am swiping on YouTube, it might be the next unpredictable video that keeps me going. If I'm in a game, it might be the next level, battle or boss.

ADHD brains are more likely to 'infinite scroll'. If you have ever been on a platform like YouTube, you have probably felt it. You are flicking through pictures and videos without really thinking, and without noticing what is around you or the time that has passed.

It is like the *empty* opposite of hyperfocus or flow. These words mean when you have an intense focus, usually on something that you enjoy doing, that can last for a long time.

The power that ADHD brains have to hyperfocus gives us a real special power. We can switch off to the world and give all our attention to learning or creating the things that matter most to us. This is amazing. It is hard to *really* get great at something, whether it is music or art, sport or writing, without being able to focus on it *entirely*.

And we ADHDers have a headstart on that. We have a skill that makes it easier for us to become

masters or *experts*, but that skill can also be a weakness. I think, like so many superpowers, it can open the door to feeling vulnerable.

Because some technology can make us *feel* like we are in hyperfocus – learning or flowing through something important – when really it is giving us an empty version of it.

Just as playing a football video game can never *quite* compare to the real-world energy and excitement of a match, or watching a YouTube video of someone at a concert can't compare to *being there* – the focus and flow we get from technology are much less.

You can have fun, but it's not the *real, deep* kind you get when you hyperfocus on something you love.

✹ DIGITAL HYPERFOCUS

Hyperfocus is a bit like eating a pudding. Pudding is great; it makes us feel good, and it is *food*, but it will make us feel bad if it is all we eat.

There is nothing wrong with playing games for a bit or getting hyperfocused on cool things online for a short time, but we have to know when to stop. Just like we know dessert can't be our *whole* dinner!

I can really enjoy a bit of time hyperfocusing on a game, and I bet other people can feel better from spending some time creating something cool on social media or seeing posts from a community they love, but we have to know when we are full.

Unlike our tummies, the tech we use doesn't really tell us when we've had enough. It's like magic ice cream that *keeps you hungry*, so you need to stop and ask yourself whether you still feel good from the time you have spent.

If you still feel energized, you've probably enjoyed some healthy hyperfocus, but if you feel tired, you might just have been staying on for too long.

✸ REWARD, NOT REPLACEMENT

I know for me, video games can *really* feel more rewarding than real life. They fit with my brain really well. I have:

- Clear goals (completing the game)

- Visible progress (levels/XP)

- Rewards for my effort (items, coins or progress)

- Satisfying sights, sounds and feedback

If I'm honest, I sometimes feel more motivated to play games than I am to do *almost anything else in my life*. But I can't always make my decisions about how I use my time *just* based on what I am feeling *right now* or what feels most satisfying in the moment.

If I did that, I would probably only play games. FOREVER.

I would become an old man one day. I would be unhealthy and probably sick. I'd have no family or friends, job, skills or achievements. I would have chosen to do the most tempting, exciting and easy thing every day. I'd have played a lot of games,

but I would have done nothing else. I'm sure you'll
agree that that doesn't sound very fun!

Because the easiest thing to do – the most
tempting one – is not usually the most satisfying.
It's the hard things that make us feel *really good*
and *learn really cool new things*.

So I try to use gaming as a reward, and not a
replacement for hard things I have to work at in my
life. If I do my work, my exercise and have good
real-world social moments with people, I am fine
to play some games.

It's a treat, like eating a pudding. And just like I
wouldn't eat ice cream and then skip breakfast,
I try and do harder things before enjoying the
low effort of games or social media.

Every household is different, but it's really important
that you all come to an agreement about when,
how often and for how long you play computer
games or go online. That way, you'll all know what
the expectations are, and you get the chance to
ask why during the discussion – and as we've
discovered, knowing the why of something makes
it much easier to follow!

To help you stick to your agreed time online or gaming, it might be a good idea to put a timer near you so you can see how much time you have left, or ask a grown-up to tell you when your time is up. They might also be able to set up time limits on your device, which can be super-helpful.

✹ SWITCHING

It's also important for me to manage gaming and social media and keep them as rewards, because then there is no risk of making them a part of my *multitasking*.

Basically, my ADHD makes me feel like I can do everything, all at once.

I am like a computer with a
thousand tabs open, jumping
between one and another,
doing little bits here and little
bits there.

That can feel satisfying, but it is
*not a good way to get things
done*. Trust me. When we try to jump
between one thing and another, we never have
the time to focus on just one and do it well. This is
really important for ADHDers. It sometimes feels
like superspeed; we can zoom from one thing to
another in a way that other people would find
confusing.

The only thing is, it's confusing for us too! We just
don't understand it. When I jump from a video
game to an app to eating, then to working, I don't
do *any of them* very well. Don't get me wrong: the
way our ADHD minds can do lots of things at once
is really useful when needed. If I am working on a
TV set, where I have to read an autocue (which is a
rolling screen of text telling me what to say), as well
as listen to someone in my headphones telling me
where to stand and think about what is happening
after the next advert break, I can do it. My brain
can do lots of things at once, and that's awesome.

✳ **HOW TO STOP SWITCHING**

But when we *only really need to do one thing*, we are much better off focusing on just that. And when we know that, we can use tools and tricks to help us do it.

Maybe you want to group similar tasks together. So if you are doing homework, *only* do homework. If you are tidying your room, focus on organizing one or two spaces (like your desk or clothes drawer), but don't also try and watch YouTube at the same time.

A more focused way of doing this is what I call 'single tab moments'. Think of it as though you are on the internet, and instead of having five tabs open, you only have one tab open. You are only focusing on one thing for a certain amount of time, and you don't want your single tab to only be used for gaming or infinite scrolling.

So think of your time and your focus in terms of twenty-minute chunks. This is where I like to use a timer. I can set a time to focus on one thing and then say, 'after twenty minutes of work, I will watch one episode,' or 'after twenty minutes of YouTube, I will tidy my room'. It's great because it saves me

from having to refocus again and again whenever I change what I am doing.

Alarms are a lot like timers, but they *remind* me of what I need to focus on rather than keep me focused on it. I have my calendar and alarms to tell me what I need to get done, and then I use my timer to make sure I can focus on doing it.

✳ BURNOUT (NO ENERGY LEFT!)

This is important when we are gaming or on social media, because in some ways, too much time can make us unwell. Our hyperfocus means we *can* get so deep into the tech we are using that we end up feeling burnt out. It's like your brain is tired from running loads of laps of the playground, but it didn't notice itself getting out of breath until it was too late. Try to learn and spot the signs of burnout, because you will feel much better if you do. Some signs are:

- Fidgeting after a long time on a screen, getting tense or having to squint

- Getting grumpy at people, or really wanting to just be alone on a screen instead of with other people

* Losing interest in all of
  the things that don't
  involve screens.

If you experience any of these,
you might be burning yourself out by using your
tech too much. Think of tech more like a mate you
chill out with for a short time, not something that
leaves you feeling tired and grumpy!

✴ ONLINE COMMUNITIES

Of course, there are *loads* of good things about
games and the internet. Just like I said at the start,
I love to chill out by playing games, and I also work
online, so I'm not here to tell you to only play with
blocks and unplug every computer in your house.
No, sir!

One great thing, particularly for ADHDers, is that
the internet can help us find information. But
remember, be careful about anything you read
about ADHD online. There are lots of good
accounts and sites out there where people share
real, helpful information, but there's a lot of fake
stuff too. Don't think that just because something
is on the internet, it is true.

And you want to be a legend leader, not a follower! You want to be someone who uses their power, rather than letting someone else use yours. So think about what you love doing – what gives you that really satisfying hyperfocus that scrolling the internet and gaming only try to recreate.

THEN DO IT.

When you do, you'll see that your ADHD is part of what makes you awesome!

CHAPTER 10
FINDING YOUR PASSION

We started this book by talking about how understanding ourselves can be the difference between ADHD feeling like a strength rather than a problem. We talked about how we can work in different and special ways and do great things if we learn to understand, explain and learn from them.

Then we looked at all the places where we can turn our differences into strengths – from school, to our friendships and family, to the food we eat and the games we play.

But there is one final way in which understanding ourselves can help us make our difference into a happier, super-er life.

And that is by finding our passion.

As I said in the last chapter, we ADHDers often have the power of hyperfocus or *flow*. This means being able to get *so into* something we love that everything else seems to disappear. Now, this special ability of ours sometimes gets us in trouble. The fact that we *love* motorbikes might be why we stare at one out of the classroom window and imagine riding it through the mountains (after we turn eighteen, of course . . .), and get told off for being distracted. Or we can get so into doodling on the edges of our homework that we end up with a whole book full of pictures of little cats and aliens and cartoon frogs, but *lots* of red marks from our teachers. Uh oh!

Don't worry, we don't need to talk any more about the weird and wonderful ways our attention span can get us in trouble. Instead, we're going to talk about how it can be a power and the best way to become great at something.

You see, lots of the famous names in history had hyperfocus and attention spans that got them in trouble. Albert Einstein (you know him – he was born in 1879, scientist, big hair, big brain, BIG GENIUS) used to get bad marks at school because he was easily distracted and

forgetful. Sound familiar? It was only
when he got older and found
something that he loved to focus on
that people realized he wasn't unfocused;
he was focused on things that interested him.

Same for the painter, sculptor and architect,
Leonardo da Vinci (born in 1452). He was another
mega-brain who people didn't really understand
because his attention and focus worked differently.
Apparently, he jumped from project to project,
leaving things unfinished and generally annoying
people around him because he worked differently.
But he also changed the world when he found
something he really wanted to focus on. Some of
his most famous works can be found in the world's
top museums today, including the *Mona Lisa*, the
most-visited painting ever, at the Louvre in Paris.

Some modern people that you might know today
who have ADHD are Dav Pilkey (the author of the
Dog Man and Captain Underpants books), Lioness
and Chelsea F.C. player Lucy Bronze, gymnastics
superstar Simone Biles, actor Emma Watson (who
played Hermione Granger in the Harry Potter
movies) and actor Tom Holland (Spider-Man!).

This different way of focusing, of searching around
for something really interesting and then going all
in, is something to appreciate. After a lifetime being

told that *I was away with the fairies* or *easily distracted*, this was a nice discovery for me.

When I realized that I didn't lack attention, that I actually had *lots of attention* that needed to find the right place, I felt relieved. Best of all, I found out that this type of attention span allows people to become really great at something.

So it's our job to find that thing – to work out what we're passionate about and *FOCUS, FOCUS, FOCUS* on it. To explain to people why we love it, why we want to focus on it over other things, and what it *feels like* for our minds to work on the thing that makes everything else disappear.

We have to find what we love to do, and then learn to love doing it well.

This might be something you have already found through learning about it in school, at a club, or through an activity outside of school.

So try and think, right now, about something you would always be happy doing.

Imagine you were left alone, in a magic world of possibility, where *any tool* was available to you. You could be given all of the paints and brushes on planet Earth by clicking your fingers, or you could be given a stage and twenty people to put on a play or the tools to start building a rocket to Mars!

If anything was possible, and there was no one telling you what you should do with your time, how would you spend it?

Because that, really, is life. You do have that power to choose what you want to focus on, then make it your goal and dream. If you are the person who daydreams about motorbikes, then you have the chance to spend your whole life learning everything there is about motorbikes. You could learn how to put them together and take them apart, how much to buy and sell them for, or what people who race them need to do to win.

If you love music – if you find you can spend hours listening to songs and making them up – then you could dedicate your life to that. You could be writing songs, performing them or helping the people who do to get their music out to more people.

The first step is to decide what you love doing.

The second is to enjoy getting better at it.

Because ADHDers focus on what is most *interesting* to us. This means we follow our passion, and in the real world, passion is a key to success.

So let's look at a few activities where passion or interest drives success, and see how ADHD can help us succeed.

✸ SPORT

Sport has always been important to me. Whether I am playing football, climbing, running or lifting weights, I feel hyperfocused when I am using my body in interesting ways.

And it is the same for lots of ADHDers. Sport can feel like the perfect match for an ADHD body and mind because it has a clear goal, a point for our energy to head towards and lots of regular boosts with points, goals or progress.

We aren't all the same, so the type of sport that we become passionate about depends on who we are. Some people like sports where the play and game moves quickly and where there are lots of small things to pay attention to all the time. Sports like basketball, football or tennis can be great for this.

If you like focusing on something slowly and trying to understand how to do something *just right*, then something like rock-climbing or a martial art might be right for you. These are sports where you have to focus very clearly on what your body is doing and repeat actions until you start to see progress. In faster-paced sports like we mentioned before, it is more about how quickly we can do the best thing possible.

Try playing a few different sports because they all need different types of thought and movement.

✳ MUSIC

You have probably seen somebody create their own tune on an instrument or freestyle with their voice. This means making music in the moment, by understanding the sounds and rhythms. This is a skill of hyperfocus.

You see, a musician isn't thinking about tidying their room or remembering their PE kit when they are

creating music. It is a time when all of their focus is in the sound. This is just one reason why many ADHDers often find music so enjoyable.

People don't know it, but I was a serious trumpet player when I was growing up – true story! I got to a high grade when I was quite young and kept playing until I was a teenager. I enjoyed it like a game – I pressed buttons and tried to achieve interesting results, and my mind found that really satisfying. (I am actually trying to start playing again, but unlike video games, you need muscles to play well – muscles in your cheeks and mouth! This is not something I've worked on at the gym . . .)

✹ DRAMA

You may remember that I mentioned some famous actors who have ADHD earlier. A lot of actors talk about their ADHD being useful for acting in plays and films. They find that their attention works well for playing a character, as they are constantly thinking, doing and *acting* in different ways. This means they have to enter a state of focus and flow, which lots of ADHDers recognize.

Performing is something I do in my life, even if I am sort of always playing myself. If I am presenting a show I find I can focus quite well on all of the different things that are going on, and feel comfortable with it, in ways that non-ADHDers might not. I like the pressure of that situation, and because my brain works better when I have to focus on something right now, rather than plan for later, I find live performance really suits me.

✳ FASHION AND DESIGN

The same goes for creating amazing things. We need a mixture of imagination and deep focus to picture something amazing and think about how to make it real.

A lot of ADHDers are *visual thinkers.* This means that we prefer to picture things in our imagination when we are thinking about how

to deal with them, rather than using numbers or words to describe them.

As we have already discussed, we also often have very strong *senses*. Patterns, textures and details, like how something feels, can be very important to ADHDers because our minds are best buddies with our senses. This is perfect for designing buildings, clothes or even things like cars, because they are not just something we live in or wear or drive – they are things we *feel*. If you think you are sensitive to these things, think about trying to design something! You might find your ADHD allows you to see and feel the world in an interesting way.

✳ HANDIWORK AND CRAFTS

Building and making things is the next step after designing them. This could mean carpentry, using wood, or mechanics (which is about connecting machines) or even designing living spaces through gardening.

These activities let us experience our work in the moment, see the

progress and connect with what we are doing. I find it difficult to focus on things that are *far in the future* and prefer to devote all my attention to what I am doing now. Creating physical things allows us to do that.

So many amazing things can be made in this way. It could be baking, building or welding. We might connect up all the lights on the Eiffel Tower or make our garden into a sea of colours. If you prefer doing something that involves problem solving and improvement, think about how you could *make* something.

Maybe start by helping in the garden or take care of some potted plants. Play with Lego or build something on Minecraft. Look in your house at how two things fit together and try to understand how someone *made that*. You might realize that you can get lost in building worlds.

✳ BUSINESS

MAKE ME A BILLIONAIRE PLEASE! OK, maybe that's a bit far, but lots of very successful, *very rich* people have ADHD. They describe how running a business means solving constant little problems, talking to people all the time and using their energy well. I like coming up with ideas and then working with people to make them real, and I've done that with two different businesses.

This is sometimes called *being an entrepreneur*. If you like challenges and the freedom to decide what you do next (independence), then this might be something you enjoy.

It is also great, because it helps with lots of the other activities we have described here. If you became a fashion designer because you love understanding how shapes and textures fit together, you could make it into a business. If you love growing plants, you could make a business out of buying and selling them or landscaping gardens.

✴ LET'S HAVE A THINK . . .

All of these hobbies and jobs are important, and they are all things that people spend their whole lives doing. They are also similar because they are not always the kinds of things we might learn at school. So many people – actors, designers, athletes and business owners – talk about how school didn't always feel easy for them. They talk about how their skills were thought of as problems when they were younger. Maybe their teachers or grown-ups just didn't understand what their passion was.

'You're daydreaming.'

This might just mean that you are imaginative, or the sort of person who will design amazing things or create new businesses.

'You're hyperactive.'

This might mean that you
have the energy it takes
to be a great sportsperson
or coach.

'You don't follow instructions.'

You could be the sort of person who sees something in a whole new way and creates something that could never have been possible if you just followed the instructions.

I know it can be hard as a kid with ADHD trying to *be the same as everyone else*, but trust me, as you get older, the world starts to celebrate people who can be different. You will not have to sit still for your whole life, or follow instructions, if you don't want to; there will be a time when energy and outside-the-box thinking are just what you need.

So try not to get down if you feel like you think differently. Don't worry if your way of working

doesn't seem to fit with primary or secondary school. Try to do your best, stay organized and be proud. You have your whole life ahead of you to use your talents and differences to achieve great things; you just need to decide what it is you love.

When you find what you love, and learn to love doing it well, you will see that the things which challenge you in school are actually what makes you amazing, just as you are.

And there is no limit to what you can achieve.

CONCLUSION

OK, brush the sparkle dust off your shoulders. Someone play the dramatic music. Get that guy who does all the voiceovers on the movie trailers to warm up. Get the special effects ready!

You have all the tools you need to make your different skills and talents work for you. I really hope you enjoyed trying out the activities and tools in this book! If found any of them particularly helpful, and you have an EHCP or formal treatment plan from a medical professional, ask whether some of these activities from the book can be added in to your plan.

Like we said, in every hero's story, there is a moment when they realize that all the things that make them different are *exactly* the things that make them strong. They have spent a long time hiding their powers, feeling awkward and different. They decided they just wanted to be like everyone else.

Then someone comes and tells them that they don't need to fit in. They need to stand out. They need to take the thing that makes them different and understand it. They need to learn how to make it useful, and decide where it can have an effect.

Instead of being angry that their superspeed makes them more likely to bump into things, they get better at controlling it and using it to do great things.

Rather than getting embarrassed that their mega-strength means they break a lot of pencils, they learn to lift buildings.

They find other people who understand them, decide where to use their power and how to explain what they are trying to do.

If you are different, then you are super. I was a hyperactive, super-chatty kid who didn't want to sit still and listen to someone talk at me.

Then I found a job and a passion where my energy was a good thing. People wanted to listen to me talk. People asked if I had any outside-of-the-box ideas. All of the things that made me think I was *stupid* became the reasons that people thought I was smart. I just had to realize that I had skills and find the places where they were useful and appreciated. I thought about it as letting my superpower shine!

So think about how your mind works. When do you feel focused and interested? How do you feel different to other people, and how could that be useful?

Then start trying different things, keep trying them and don't stop until you find something that makes you MEGA-happy. If you discover something you could do forever, without anyone telling you to sit down and concentrate, you've found your goal and your passion.

You have the power to work differently and do great things. You don't have to wear your pants outside your trousers and act like a superhero. Or even save the world.

You just have to enjoy it in the way that works for you.

Stay super.

Sam

If you and your grown-ups would like to find out more about ADHD, and find some more ways to help, try checking out some UK charity websites such as ADHD UK and ADDISS (ADHD Information Services).

GLOSSARY

ADHD: stands for **Attention Deficit Hyperactivity Disorder**. People with ADHD have differences in how their brain develops and works.

ADHDers: people who have been diagnosed with ADHD.

Balanced: having the right, even or fair amount of different things so nothing is too heavy, too much or too little.

Energized: feeling super-awake, active and ready to play or do something fun!

Gamify: to do an everyday activity like doing homework, tidying your room or learning maths and add game-like rules to make it fun, exciting and more engaging.

Hyperfocus: when your brain is really focused on something you enjoy, making you feel like you are in your own world or 'in the zone'.

Hypersensitive: your senses (sight, hearing, touch, smell and taste) are like a super-sensitive volume button. For a lot of people, the world is at volume five. For you, the world might feel like it is turned up to ten. A hug might feel too tight, a small noise might feel like a shout, and scratchy clothing might feel painful.

Overwhelmed: when you might have too many thoughts and feelings at a time in your day, and you might feel that sitting still is tough or doing an activity at school is hard.

Regulation: a process that helps you understand and be the boss of your own emotions, to help you feel calm.

Rejection sensitivity disorder: having upsetting and strong emotions that are caused by a worry of rejection or failing.

Sensitivity: having a 'super-powered' nervous system that might feel, hear and notice more than others.

Sensory: how our bodies use the five main senses (sight, sound, smell, taste and touch) to explore and understand the world.

Spiral: a quick, overwhelming rise of negative emotions or behaviours that become difficult to deal with.

ACKNOWLEDGEMENTS

I want to thank my family, friends and colleagues for supporting my journey with ADHD (and Autism) and loving me just as I am. Your unwavering support before, during and after my diagnosis means the world to me.

I want to thank Dr Jessica Eccles, who diagnosed me in 2023 – you were a key part of my journey.

A big thank you to Channel 4, South Shore and Sophie Wright for making my documentary *Is This ADHD?*

I also want to thank the team at ADHD UK for making me Ambassador of such a great charity that does a brilliant job in raising funds and awareness.

I want to thank my amazing team at Puffin for helping to bring this book to life. Fenella, Jessie, Sarah, Nell, Naomi, Phoebe, Sonia, Lottie – this book literally wouldn't exist without you all. I hope it will help many young people.

I need to give a special shout-out to Oscar Millar, who helped me get my words onto the page – that's not easy, so thank you! And a mention of gratitude to the professionals who helped us with specific neurodivergent information and content.

My team – Seb, Jonny, Charlotte and Megan – thank you for everything you do for me. Another brilliant project we can all be proud of.

And most of all I want to thank the British public. From the moment I spoke about my ADHD in *I'm A Celebrity. . . Get Me Out Of Here!*, I've received nothing but support. I've met so many of you and had thousands and thousands of messages thanking me for being so honest about my neurodiversity. But it's YOU who I need to thank – the warmth and encouragement over the past few years from the public has led me to living an authentic, happy life, and ultimately to create this book.